A Piece of My Heart I Leave Behind

DIANA JANSE

A Piece of My Heart
I Leave Behind

Translated by Sonia Wichmann

Layout: BoD – Books on Demand
Printing: BoD – Books on Demand, Stockholm, Sweden
Production: BoD – Books on Demand, Norderstedt, Germany
ISBN: 978-91-7851-715-2

Original title: En del av mitt hjärta lämnar jag kvar
First published in Sweden by Alfabeta in 2010

TABLE OF CONTENTS

Preface

In 2004, the Swedish Ministry for Foreign Affairs established a new position at the embassy in Islamabad, Pakistan, with placement in Kabul, Afghanistan, at the local headquarters of Sida (the Swedish International Development Cooperation Agency). It was hard to find candidates who were willing to go there. When the job was announced for the third time, it caught my eye. Before I even realized what had happened, I had applied for the job, been accepted, and was on my way.

I had worked at the Ministry for Foreign Affairs since 1999; I had been posted in Moscow and had also worked in Belgrade and New York. The year before I went to Kabul, I was a desk officer at the European Security Department in Stockholm. It was an unglamorous and stressful job that entailed working at my desk from early morning until late evening, writing instructions for our negotiators at the European Union delegation in Brussels. For the first time since my dream of becoming a diplomat was born, in the shabby student housing on the outskirts of Moscow where I was living in the early 1990s, I doubted my choice of career. This was not what I had had in mind. But then what did I have in mind? Restlessness churned inside me.

I can't say exactly why I applied for the job in Kabul, or why I accepted it when it was offered to me. Maybe it was just chance, or maybe it was a rebellion against the boring dinner parties and lifestyle magazines that were the backdrop of my daily life. Maybe the endless writing of instructions had drained so much satisfaction out of my work that I was ready to try something different – anything – a dream of adventure and a naive but sincere wish to do something, to make a difference. Maybe it was just an example of my poor judgment. Maybe I longed to engage in something more urgent, more universally human. To see, to learn, to understand. Or maybe just to start over. And maybe it was all of these reasons mixed together. I can make up some good reasons now, in hindsight, but I don't really know. Some decisions simply make themselves.

I had traveled through much of Asia, and I had lived and worked for a year in a country that was engulfed in war, but Afghanistan was a blank page for me. To my mind, our engagement in Afghanistan is about security and about countering the threat that Islamic extremism poses to our western democracies. But above all, it is about better living conditions for millions of Afghans, and about basic humanitarian values. Gandhi once said that poverty is the worst form of violence. How can an entire nation be lifted out of poverty? No one knows the answer, but it certainly isn't through aid alone. Aid works – or doesn't work – in a context. Development and the eradication of poverty cannot be isolated from their political, cultural, economic, geographic, or security contexts, to name a few factors.

In a vain attempt to prepare myself, I read some books on my vacation in the weeks before my departure. *Like preparing yourself for starvation when you have never experienced hunger.* I booked a ticket, packed my bags. It would just have to turn out however it was going to turn out.

These are some fragments of my story. My book is part documentary, part journal. I'm writing about real events and real people. As always when dealing with a selection of material, the result will be a skewed picture of reality. Other people would remember different events and different details, and have different interpretations. My intent has been to write about what I saw, experienced, heard, and thought – a small part of everything that I carry with me after almost two years in Afghanistan. It was a time that made my world so much bigger and more remarkable, and that has shaped me and my view of the world, my work, my friends, and my context more than I could ever have imagined. If it has also made me pretentious, or if I have offended anyone, I hope my readers will forgive me.

Give me courage to live
before I die.

ANONYMOUS

The Bottom of the World
[September 2004]

A carpet of parched brown mountains spreads out under the scorching sun. Through the small window of the plane, it looks like velvet draped over the mountainsides. No roads, only mountains, mountains, and more mountains that reach toward the intense blue sky. The last thing I see before we land is the plane wrecks that line the runway, and the veins of weeds running through the cracked asphalt. With a light thud, the tiny propeller plane touches down. We taxi toward the low terminal building and the engines come to a stop. One of the pilots wriggles out of his seat. Hunched over as he stands inside the cabin, he welcomes us to Kabul's international airport. The door opens, and a small stairway is folded out. It has taken me more than 24 hours to get here, but now, finally, I have arrived.

Ingela is waiting for me in the terminal building, leaning against a pillar.

"Welcome to Kabul," she says.

The sharp sunlight pushes through the dingy glass doors in the terminal building, revealing the unwashed floors of the hall and the weathered faces of the men around us who are watching us with curiosity. Yes, welcome to the bottom of the world.

The car ride to the Wazir Akbar Khan neighborhood takes perhaps 10 minutes. Ingela, this fidgety stranger sent by Sida, talks nonstop. It sounds like she's on speed. We have never met before, but have spoken on the phone a few times. She has been here for a few months, and now we are colleagues. And housemates as well – she's offered to let me stay in her guest room until I find a place of my own. I look at her sideways from my seat in the back. Her lips are moving, she's waving her hands around, tossing back her long hair, rolling her eyes, keeping one eye on the road and the driver, one on me. I don't hear a word of what she's saying. Instead, as I sit there I'm trying to rouse the feeling of adventure and escapism that made me come here – or rather, made me voluntarily ask to come here. But that feeling will not come back even for one second. Instead, only a pathetic self-pity wells up. What have I done? What was wrong with my old Stockholm neighborhood, anyway? A little shabby, perhaps, but everything is relative. All in all, it's pretty nice. And Martin. The feeling of missing him stabs at me. What wouldn't I give just to be with him now! What was I thinking? What on earth was I thinking? Back then, my dream was to leave behind the boredom that was frittering away my energy and wellbeing. My dream was to disappear from the census like in an Orwell novel. To be able to start over. Tabula rasa. But this? It's unfathomable. I look at my new hometown through the car window as we roll by, and I struggle with a feeling of dejection and the gnawing sense of having made a huge mistake. Some lines from a Belle and Sebastian song have gotten stuck in my brain:

The future's looking colorful.
It's the color of blood, chaos, and corruption of a happy soul.

I take a few deep breaths in the backseat. I smile, nod in agreement toward Ingela as she gesticulates away. It's as if someone has muted the sound in a movie. I have no idea what this person is talking about. All of my self-pity has settled like cotton in my ears.

A New Morning

It's the beginning of September, 2004, and my first week at work. Just like a cockroach, I soon adjust to my new surroundings. On Tuesday I have stomach flu; on Wednesday, we have a car accident on the short stretch home from work; on Thursday there's a rocket attack on the neighborhood next to us and we hunker down in Ingela's house, which has no cellar or shelter. I brush it off just as I brush off the brown dust that settles over everything like a fine membrane. It feels like I've been released from a straitjacket. What a relief to be able to move again! I knew that something had been constricting me and chafing at me, but I hadn't understood the reason why: I felt stuck in a morass of non-essentials. And now, suddenly – a new world around me, a sense of urgency, challenge, and adventure. Wherever I look I'm forced to think, to understand new relationships, to stretch my limits. And all the people around me – their curious, cautious looks and their smiles make me feel warm.

Nothing has been prepared for my arrival – no workspace, no functioning computer, no housing. But I do have a telephone. The head of Sida in Afghanistan hasn't exactly made a secret of the fact that he doesn't want some stuck-up diplomat in *his* office. He has openly worked against me from the very start. I don't take it personally. The rivalry between the Ministry for Foreign Affairs and Sida can take such petty forms; it is as well-known and institutionalized as it is tiresome. Still, I appreciate the fact that he's straightforward about it, although a little politeness would have lightened the atmosphere. I let him be. Nothing really gets to me, least of all some mean-spirited old official.

Once I've cleaned up the room that will be my office, and set up the computer, I turn to my work – political reporting – with unbridled enthusiasm. Soon there will be a presidential election and Afghanistan will turn over a page in its soiled history book. The country's future is like clay on the potter's wheel, just waiting to be shaped into something better and brighter. I learn everything about election laws, organization, ballot counting, and logistics. I try to understand what is happening, how the Islamic state under Pashtun dominance that we are helping to build is going to hold together. At this point, nothing is working. Not the electric power, not the factories, not communications. And above all, not the state. President Karzai rules the country as carelessly as a wolf guards the sheep. Corruption and mismanagement wreak havoc right and left.

And I try to understand what has happened in the past. A hundred years after the so-called Great Game, the British and Russian race for influence in Central Asia, it is business as usual, only with more expensive playthings and higher stakes. Iran, Pakistan, Russia, India, China, USA – they all have their agendas, barely hidden in the sand. Afghanistan's own interests never seem to be part of the political equation. Behind windows covered with safety film, I dig around in the sediment of history. Who fought against whom twenty years ago? Which country financed which warlord? Who belongs to which tribe? A tangled picture emerges, made up of interwoven intrigues, betrayal, and espionage.

When Hamid Karzai was appointed chairman of the Interim Administration in December 2001, and later, Interim President, he became a symbol of the civilized regime that took over Afghanistan after the barbaric Taliban. With his lambskin hat and his green kaftan, he lent a suitably exotic flavor to the halls of power. He looked good on CNN. Well-spoken and charismatic, he took the world by storm, and Tom Ford at Gucci dubbed him "the chicest man on the planet". But up close, it's hard not to see how the fashionable facade is peeling away. The rooster on the dungheap, his detractors call him with a chuckle. Others mock him as "the mayor of Kabul", exposing his scanty influence beyond the walls of the palace that he shares with the old king, Zahir Shah, who recently returned from Rome after decades in exile, now with the title Father of the Nation. Somehow the fact that the country has both a president and a king sums up the essence of Afghanistan's politics – constant compromises, strange alliances, and a state machinery that is oversized in relation to its influence. Two Afghans make three political factions, people tell me with a laugh.

President Karzai's own political career illustrates how alliances are formed and broken with a light touch here in the struggle for power and influence. Hamid Karzai belongs to the influential Popalzai clan, one of the clans in the Durrani tribe. Durrani Pashtuns ruled Afghanistan from 1747 until 1973, when the monarchy was overthrown. Karzai's father, Abdul Ahad Karzai, was the leader of the Popalzai clan and held government posts in Kabul under King Zahir Shah, who ruled the country for forty years before being ousted in a bloodless coup in 1973. When the Soviets invaded, the family fled to Quetta, in Pakistan. The future president himself eventually joined the side of the Mujahedin movement that resisted Soviet occupation, while his brothers emigrated to the United States, where they opened a number of Afghan restaurants. When the communist-friendly regime fell in 1992, Karzai became Vice Foreign Minister in President Rabbani's government, but he resigned in 1994. When the Taliban came to power in 1996, he briefly allied himself with them. In 1997, he returned to Quetta and along with his father, joined the opponents of the Taliban. When his father was murdered in 1999, Karzai became the leader, or *khan*, of the Popalzai clan's approximately 500,000 members. In 2001, when the Taliban were toppled from power and retreated into the mountains, he returned to Kabul, now as interim leader, backed by the United States. Karzai's earlier cooperation with the Taliban, among others, is now hushed up, an embarrassing parenthesis that people seem to want to forget.

During the years that have passed since Karzai became interim president, his constant alliance-building, maneuvering, and unwillingness to get on the wrong side of first one group, then another – whether jihadists or Taliban, Westerners or influential neighbors – have turned the everyday political reality into a balancing act on a tightrope. *Keep your friends close, but your enemies closer.* It seems that by creating ties to his enemies, he hopes he might just possibly be able to control them. He promises first one thing, then the opposite. Says this, but does that. Or says both this and that, but does nothing. As the months go by, the web of alliances, agreements, and promises of government positions becomes so tightly woven that he no longer has any room to maneuver. But here, people, rather than actual policies, are what matter.

At the end of my first week, I'm walking home. The gravel crunches under my shoes, and the sunshine is so bright it makes my eyes ache. In the short stretch to the house where I live, I pass some forty security guards, dressed in threadbare uniforms and slippers, watching the houses and the Chinese bordellos along the way. I greet them.

"*Asal'amu aleykum!*"

"*W'aleykum asal'am*", they respond, raising one hand in the air, sometimes all the way up to a worn hat brim.

For a minute, their smiles erase the deep lines of weariness and resignation from their faces. They swing their Kalashnikovs jauntily and regard me with curiosity, as if I've landed from outer space with some interplanetary time machine. And in some ways I have, so vast is the difference in our life circumstances.

Sightseeing [October 2004]

It's Friday and a day off, the only day off in the week. On my way to Chicken Street, Kabul's main shopping street, I pass a group of men on their way to Friday prayer. They are dressed in freshly washed, well ironed *shalwar kamiz*, long cotton shirts with pajama-like pants. The men walk quickly, leaning slightly forward and with their gaze fixed on the ground. They seem to be in a hurry; I wonder if maybe they are examining their lives, or maybe they're thinking about what they can do to make Allah give them a more bearable life. An older man in the group picks up his feet a little higher as he walks, as if to urge on the too-large plastic sandals that hang from them, only reluctantly allowing themselves to be dragged along to the mosque. The call to prayer has already begun. *Allah Akbar!* Allah is greatest.

"Breaking news, five times a day," I once heard someone remark drily.

Kabir parks the white Land Cruiser. I ask him to wait, and jump out of the car, closing the door behind me. Chicken Street is a short street, bordered by dismal heaps of trash and an open sewer that runs between the street and the sidewalk. I walk down the street with no particular plan in mind, among the small shops selling jewelry, shawls, rugs, and mirrors. I enter one of the rug shops and sift absently through the piles. It feels good not to have to make so many choices all the time. Between milk with 2% fat and 1%, between energy from Fortum or Vattenfall. Here in Afghanistan, I'm just happy if I happen to have an hour or two of electricity sometimes.

Finally I settle on a small doormat that depicts a plane crashing into the Twin Towers. It reads "Afghanistan 2001" at the lower edge. It captures today's Afghanistan, a creative fusion of tradition and violence.

"*Qimat 'in chand ast?*" I ask the man who has been following my growing interest with satisfaction.

He fingers his prayer beads, a little faster now, not quite as distractedly as before.

"You are a guest here in this country. *Khosh 'amadid!* How long have you been here? Where do you come from?"

The man is smiling from head to toe. I guess that he is a Tajik, with his fine features and clear blue eyes.

"I'm from Sweden. But how much is the rug?" I repeat.

I point to the handwoven Boeing 767 with its nose wedged in the glass and concrete.

"The price is unimportant. Would you like some tea?"

I take aim again.

"What does it cost?"

The man turns to a boy in a white *shalwar kamiz* and a downy moustache. He's wearing a white cap on his head with little mirrors embroidered on it. The man gives a few orders. Before the boy disappears inside the store he turns to me.

"Green or black?"

I brace myself with patience that I really don't have.

"How much does it cost?" I repeat, and take two steps, small but threatening, toward the exit.

"Fifty dollars."

He smiles, not only with his mouth and his gray teeth, but with his whole body.

"For you, my friend and guest of Afghanistan, only fifty dollars. You are my first customer today. You are getting a good price."

I laugh harshly and point to the small, ugly doormat.

"I'll give you twenty dollars."

The man rolls his eyes and the corners of his mouth turn down.

"It's the first time you are here in my store!"

"Twenty dollars," I repeat.

"Impossible! I myself paid forty-five dollars for it!"

Three, maybe, I think to myself. Or maybe five. The truth is elastic here, something that you stretch to suit your needs until it has completely lost its meaning. But I still want the rug. I've already remodeled not only the entryway in my Stockholm apartment, but my entire world around it. The caption in some future "At home with..." feature in the Swedish magazine *Beautiful Homes* appears before my eyes with exceptional clarity: "*In her home, fragments of the nomadic life meet Scandinavian minimalism. The ironic doormat was purchased in Kabul.*" I'm in the photo next to it, dressed in an elegant pantsuit, and holding a vase (Alvar Aalto, of course) with red tulips. I'm smiling, one of those smiles that good people smile, and I'm slim as a pencil line.

"I'll give you twenty dollars, no more."

"For twenty dollars, you can have this rug," he says, tugging a motheaten rag out of a pile.

I stroke the soft, dense pile of the rug, tracing one of the twin towers from top to bottom.

"But I'm only talking about this one. Not any other one. I'm not interested in any other rug."

The boy with the downy moustache comes back and serves me tea in a dirty cup, along with some candies in colorful wrappers.

"What do you want it for?"

"What difference does that make?"

"What's your best price?"

"My best and only price is twenty dollars," I repeat again.

"Impossible! I've given you a friend price! Forty-five dollars. Then I won't make any profit myself."

And we continue like that. In the end, there's no rug. There's no *Beautiful Homes* article. I will never be beautiful, happy, or thin.

With heavy steps but head held high – that's the least I can do – I leave the shop and continue down the street. No matter what I do, I can't blend into the cityscape. I don't even try. With the exception of one beggar dressed in a ragged, baby blue burka, there are no women for me to blend in with. The beggar stretches her chapped, dirty hand toward me. It's impossible to meet her eyes. Instead, I pretend not to see her, like an ice cube in a glass of water. But I feel her gaze following me – pleading, accusing, and filled with the sorrow of life's unfairness. A man with greased hair and reptilian brain shouts the few English words he knows, first a guttural "Hello!" and then a bolder "I love you". I fix my gaze far away and pretend not to hear him. *This is my world too,* I want to say, but don't. It wouldn't make any difference. This is not my world, nor is it the Afghan women's world. Here in

Afghanistan, as I once heard then vice foreign minister Haider Reza declare, a woman is worth half a man.

"Those are the words of God in the Koran and nothing can change them," he added.

But if we only had half the world, that would be plenty.

When I've grown tired of the shops and the searching gazes of the Afghan men, I go sightseeing. Leaning back against the jeep's vinyl seat, I watch the city roll by. Summer has lingered on; the merciless rays of the sun cut like lasers through the dinginess of Afghan poverty. Nearly a quarter of a century of senseless war has left reminders everywhere – Kabul is a city that fell over the edge of ruin long ago. If you are used to being surrounded by objects chosen with care and taste, used to a well-proportioned, aesthetically planned milieu, well, then this is the wrong place to come. Even though almost three years have passed since the fall of the Taliban, there are few signs of progress here. No seductive advertising signs, no new stretches of road, no cafés, no attractive shops for the nouveau riche. There aren't even any street signs, only dust and broken kiosks with shabby facades, selling imported chocolate bars that have turned gray. The few buildings that once had a bit of style have lost it decades ago. For the most part, the houses are made of mud brick, the same rug-brown color as the mountainsides on which they are perched. The houses at the top look like swallows' nests, clinging to the slope in defiance of gravity. I can't help but wonder where all the money that has been pumped into the land – a mind-boggling fourteen billion dollars – has disappeared to. Dubai? Switzerland?

Along Butcher Street, cut-up animal carcasses hang from hooks outside the stalls. There's a sweet smell, and flies buzz in the air. Here you can buy a *murg-e shahid*, a martyr chicken. After all, who wants to die in vain – even if you're a chicken? Why die an ordinary unglamorous, meaningless death, when you can die a martyr's death?

The car makes its way between donkey carts and decrepit, saffron-yellow Corolla taxis. It is crowded, always crowded, on the few dilapidated roads that haven't yet been closed for security reasons, on the streets where you are allowed to pass even if you don't belong to ISAF (International Security Assistance Force), the Nato-led international force, or have a car with diplomatic plates. And for each incident or attack it grows a little more crowded – a few more concrete blocks are put in place, a new road barrier set up, yet another road closed off, yet one more place ends up on the list of areas not considered safe enough for foreigners to visit. The bunker mentality is reinforced even more, the distance between us and the people for whose sake we are here increases. The only ones who benefit from it are the extremists – the Taliban, or terrorists, or others who don't want us foreigners here.

We pass the Olympic stadium with its rusting Olympic rings, where the Taliban used to hold public executions on Fridays during the glory days of the Islamic Emirate Afghanistan. Homosexuals were buried alive, murderers were shot, and adulterous women were stoned to death.

"Everyone went there!" My driver, Kabir, laughs. His glance meets mine in the rearview mirror. His eyes are always red; whether from all the cigarettes he smokes, or because they've just seen too much blood and sorrow, I don't know.

Kabir is one of the three drivers for the office. He is a Pashtun, and the only one I've met who spent the whole war in the country and not in a refugee camp in Pakistan or Iran. He is overqualified for his job – he's smart, and sharp as a weasel, and he speaks Dari, Pashto, English, and Urdu. Other circumstances would have made something different of Kabir, but now he sits here behind the wheel, navigating around his tattered homeland, year after year. And always with a smile to spare.

We drive past the Kabul River, a muddy riverbed covered in stinking garbage, where some women are sitting in their prisons of cloth, apparently washing clothes. Then we turn towards the devastated part of the city called *Kart-e Seh*. Kilometers of ruins roll past through the film of dust on the window. Kabir's favorite cassette is playing on the tape player in the car, or maybe it's just his only cassette, a painful sound background by Stevie Wonder and Wham: *I just called to say I love you*. For a moment, my thoughts turn to Martin and the echoing silence that has spread out between us since I came here. But only for a moment. Then I force my gaze out through the window again. One arduous meter at a time registers in my brain to the swooning tones of the music. Buildings and mud houses in all shapes – with three walls and a collapsed roof, with one wall and no roof, and countless variations on the same theme. This part of the city looks like it has gone through a stone crusher, like a post-apocalyptic scene in a science fiction movie. It's a scene of destruction that reminds me of the photos of Dresden in my old history book, although here they are colored brown and gray, with moving, emaciated donkeys.

In the 1960s and 1970s, this area was flourishing. With its liberal milieu and its cheap drugs, the city attracted travelers – hippies, flower power-people – from near and far. Back then, this was the handsomest neighborhood in Kabul, with tree-lined avenues, parks, and foreign missions. Now it's home to the poorest of the poor, who move around wearily, as if their pockets were filled with stones.

At the very end of the road, the climax of our sightseeing awaits: the bombed-out royal palace in Darul Aman. What remains of the palace roof has caved in, and as for the walls, only some of the supporting beams remain, along with enough of the masonry to be able to see that the building was once yellow. On the other side of the road is the National Museum, which used to house one of the most significant art treasures of Central Asia – stupas with reliefs, clay pots, clothing from several centuries, Persian manuscripts with exquisite calligraphy – but that was before the Taliban destroyed thousands of the artifacts.

Some NATO soldiers have set up a lookout post in the palace ruins. It's a mystery to me what they are watching out for. We drive around the palace and then roll back toward town. This is war tourism in its most perverted form – *Disaster Travel's number one for value*. But there's nothing else to see in my new hometown.

Long-Distance Relationship

"When are you coming?" I ask for at least the tenth time. "Have you arranged your visa?"

I try to entice him by telling him about a Thai restaurant I've found just a few blocks from home, and the pleasant fall weather; with anecdotes about the upcoming presidential election; with all the excursions to be made in the region. Maybe we could drive north, to Mazar-e Sharif. Or to Islamabad. Or to Bamian. Or just stay in Kabul. I tell him about all the people I've already gotten to know, about politics, about everyday life. For a journalist like him, there's endless material to write about here. There's so much to talk about that the words come bubbling out.

"I don't know," Martin answers.

I can almost hear him squirm.

It isn't easy to commute between Kabul and Stockholm. It's expensive, it's far, it's complicated to get any insurance company to work with you. *Sorry, we do not insure burning houses.* But the warning that I've heard since day one at the MFA, that it's hard to make private life and career work together in this line of work, that has never really been an issue for us. We were above all that, we waved it away. We were modern. Equal. It would work out somehow. In the beginning, I would travel and he would come here and visit, stay for a month or two. Then we would have to work out some kind of plan. It was simple. And after all, I had only committed myself to being away for one short year.

But now everything is teetering.

"It's so hard to arrange it, I don't know ..."

Of course I can hear that he doesn't want to come. But I want him to come. Once he's here, I know he'll like it. Don't all journalists dream of a trench coat, a spiralbound notebook and the Great Adventure? *Voilà*, here it is, served up on a platter.

No normal, bright person could prefer a life within the borders when the whole world lies at our feet. Once released from the chains of comfort...

"What do you mean, you don't know?" I almost have to shout over the bad connection.

"I have so much work. And the new record…"

I don't say anything. *Yes, and…?*

"And we're going on tour, and then…"

I don't know how many of his band's concerts I've been to, and I've truly loved them. But after a hundred, is it really still as important to have a hundred more? Can't he skip at least ten of them? Five? Eight?

"But not every weekend, though? You can get away for a couple of weeks, can't you? You could take your guitar and laptop with you, work here. Or take the whole band with you."

The connection breaks up, for the umpteenth time in a row. I hang up and dial again.

"It really is fantastic in spite of everything. You'd like it, if you only came, met the Afghans, saw for yourself. It's exciting! Different. Believe me," I plead.

OK, don't come then. You just sit there in your tour bus on the road between Västerås and Eskilstuna and sulk. Your loss.

Ikea Goes to Kabul [October 2004]

Fall has definitely arrived now; the air has grown colder. I've found a small house a few blocks from the office and have started to put my things in order. It's taken a while. I've looked at more houses than I can count, each one odder than the one before.

After the Taliban disappeared, there was a booming business in renting out insanely expensive houses to the thousands of aid workers and diplomats who were streaming into the country. Real estate prices were higher in Kabul than in Tokyo and New York. But now the market is saturated, or at least the supply doesn't match the demand. In the Wazir Akbar Khan district there must be fifty or so sprawling, newly built houses, unrented. Who wants to live in a 28-room house with ten bathrooms – all with pearly pink, shell-shaped sinks, but without a parking spot or garden? Or in garish two-, three-, or four-story houses with decorated balconies and facades made of multicolored glass and mirrored mosaic, with towers and carved railings and unclear ownership? My wishes are more modest, and my budget as well. My cockroaches and I can easily fit into the house that I've found, behind a dingy grayish-white wall: a living room with a fireplace where I never manage to light a proper fire, a kitchen and toilet on the first floor, four small rooms and a bathroom on the second floor. For over four thousand dollars a month. That does not include a generator, furniture, lamps, heat, or electricity; there's no stove, refrigerator, or freezer in the kitchen; and no washing machine in the bathroom, with its 1960s decor. It is a shell with four walls and a roof, and a miserable little patch of grass in front of the house. *Special price, only for me.*

After a great deal of bureaucracy, paper, and rubber stamps; certificates, powers of attorney, and violent verbal exchanges, my things are finally allowed through customs. Some young men carry my moving boxes, containing a few books, linens, CDs, kitchen things, and clothes, into the empty house, along with some Ikea furniture that a kind administrator in Stockholm has decided I should have. Then the men spend days screwing together the furniture from the parts in the flat packages, sitting cross-legged on my living room floor, mesmerized. After a week or two everything is in order. However ugly the furniture may be, and however cold the stone floors, it's my home. Home! Me in a house.

Malalai, a widow with four children to support, offers to help with the housecleaning.

"My husband – dead!" she explains, making an imaginary cut across her throat with one hand. "Taliban."

Malalai loves to cook, and in the beginning I let her. Plates of food are waiting for me in the refrigerator when I come home. For some mysterious reason, everything that she prepares tastes exactly the same. And even though I use an interpreter, she can't quite understand – or accept – the concept of being vegetarian. Time and again I point accusingly to the small pieces of meat that find their way into the pasta and pies and into my bowl of soup. So small that they hardly count. So small that I shouldn't be able to find them. After a few weeks, I give up. She will have to limit herself to doing laundry and cleaning. It never gets very clean, but it is what it is. It doesn't get any better than this. This is the land of 17 percent, and I try to learn to ramp down my ambitions. And I'm happy that I've actually employed a wage-earning woman in my household. There aren't many of those hereabouts.

Us and Them [October 2004]

It's a beautiful, long, sunny fall. Together with my new-found European friends, I've created a parallel world for myself in the midst of the Afghan wretchedness. We are all in the same boat – our jobs have brought us here, we've left friends and family behind, we seek each other out in the little free time that's left after work. As I move between the two worlds, reports about the increasing number of suicide bombers and kidnappings whisper in my ear: *Memento mori, memento mori.* Grill parties, restaurant visits, and movie nights at home follow one after the other, right in the middle of a humanitarian catastrophe zone, a country that is slowly bleeding to death, an existence completely removed from the one that I've left behind. In this place there are no organized pension plans, no baby carriages, and no hissing, shiny espresso machines.

But it's a harder task to make contacts with the Afghan people. When I lived in Moscow, I made an effort to get to know Russians and to create a Russian context for myself. I look desperately for ways to break through into the daily life and reality of the Afghan people, but find that I more or less have to give up. Afghan men don't associate with women, and the Afghan women are nearly invisible.

Even if I were to knock on some wooden door and find a woman my age, what would I have in common with a mother of nine, married off at age 14, who has never set foot in a school? What human experiences do we share? What specifically female experiences? My exile is self-inflicted. I can book a flight away from here whenever I want, and 24 hours later turn the key in the door of my apartment in Stockholm, which has electricity, water, a comfortable room temperature, and a remodeled kitchen. So what can I reasonably expect to understand, with my money, my EuroBonus points, and my twenty years of education? Could I understand their life conditions? Their dreams? Their fears? Maybe that's why we can't figure out this country. We simply know too little, we don't understand even half of what's going on.

The closest I come is to meet with some of the many Afghans who grew up in the United States and have now come here, many for the first time, to work for the UN or some aid organization. The Afghans tend to regard returnees with suspicion – especially those who fled during the many long, difficult years, who have now returned and acquired influential positions in the steadily swelling state apparatus. I don't think they are considered "real" Afghans.

It's Thursday evening in a foreign country. I'm sitting at the bar at the Elbow Room, waiting for Nick, a British colleague. The Elbow Room is Afghanistan's version of Rick's Café Américain. In spite of its shabbiness, the place holds a baffling attraction for the city's flock of foreigners. The air is thick with smoke and aid jargon. In an endless stream of fleeting encounters, we deafen our senses and exchange observations with an overtone of colonialism, as we wait to move on to the next postcolonial experimental workshop. Maybe Darfur. Or Iraq, for those with a real death wish. We are all employed by different affiliates of Catastrophe Inc, an enterprise that follows the weapons industry at its heels, on its crusade around the world.

It's mostly men in the bar, former soldiers in civilian clothes, employed in the ever expanding security industry. These are men who never want to talk about what they do, because they seem so much more interesting if they just give a vague answer. Men who were probably well trained and fit two thousand beers ago. Still, they look like they are headed out on an expedition in the Himalayas as soon as they've emptied their glasses, with their boots, North Face shirts, and pants with too many pockets. But now there's a girl standing next to me at the bar, with a startling orange-brown skin tone and the most extravagant clothes. She looks like she's from the celebrity magazine *Veckans NU!*, maybe someone in Paris Hilton's circle of acquaintances. She's wearing a pair of figure-hugging pants with a big flashy belt buckle and dozens of necklaces. Her top is tight and bares her abdomen. I wonder if she packed a whole solarium with her, while I only managed to bring extra-warm longjohns and hand sanitizer gel.

She looks at me and an uncertain expression crosses her face. "Didn't we meet last year? In East Timor?"

A not too far-fetched opening line, the catastrophe industry's variation on "Do you come here often?"

I shake my head.

"What are you doing here?" she asks, already uninterested in my answer.

Sandy has been in the country for five months. She has only one month left in her contract with some aid organization that distributes apples, or schoolbooks, or runs embroidery courses for Afghan women. I can't really remember; I wasn't interested in the answer.

Sandy tosses her blonde hair like in *Flashdance* and complains about the traffic, the food, and the weather. She doesn't fit my image of an aid worker – no comfortable shoes, straight-laced clothing, or naturally rosy cheeks. No enthusiasm for the genuine, the real, or the true in the local culture, values that must be preserved at any price.

"So you don't like living in Afghanistan," I finally say when she stops talking for a minute to sip her drink.

"I love it!"

She takes another swig of the sticky cocktail in her glass and looks at me with her wide open, expertly made-up cow eyes. I wonder if she might be on some kind of drug.

"But it will be nice to move on soon. I'm going to Liberia."

The dream of starting over again – it's so sweet, so enticing, and it's so deceptively easy to get caught in its web. There, somewhere else, you will finally do the things that you could never get around to doing here, become the person you always wanted to be, the person you were meant to be. Beautiful, successful, happy. Good. Productive and well-spoken. Why not famous and slim, too? But all that happens is that your belongings are damaged in the move. All that's left of your high hopes is a daily, ongoing struggle: To find someone who can sell you a little bread and something you can prepare for dinner. To not get lost, to at least find your way home and to work, zig-zagging between the hellish potholes in the roads. To find someone who can explain where to put the garbage, and how the generator works. You are so busy trying to survive that there's no time left over to be productive or good. You barely have time to wash your hair.

But on the other side of the balance is the incredible satisfaction of finding a packet of Philadelphia cream cheese among all the nuts, canned tomatoes, and boxes of couscous, or managing to say a few words in a foreign tongue and actually making yourself understood. Pure, total joy.

Sandy tosses her shining mane some more and complains that all the people here are so ugly and untrendy. I swallow some of my sour red wine. I can allow for some complaining about the violence and misogyny and all the shattered lives – but what did she expect?

"Oh yes, Liberia," I mumble. "I heard that they've opened a Jimmy Choo shop in Monrovia."

"What? Really?"

For the first time, she looks genuinely interested.

"What? No, it was nothing ..."

A man with a crew cut and a t-shirt two sizes too small, the sleeves stretched tight around his arm muscles, is calling for her attention. His veins run like ropes along his arms; soon she's captivated by his fairy dust.

I'm left standing alone at the bar. I look out over the room. To be honest, this is a sad place. Had it been in Sweden, I would never have set foot in it. Still, I can't help but like it; it's a little corner of something else, something that reminds me of Europe and that I need to see sometimes in order to want to stay here.

MOT Golf [November 2004]

Captain Kim meets me at a military tent camp near the airport in Mazar-e Sharif. He is the group leader of MOT Golf, the Swedish military observation team with whom I am to ride around for a few days in northern Afghanistan. Kim looks genuinely happy to see me. He is energetic as he explains everything that needs to be done before we can set out. The men in the group need to shower, change clothes, eat a solid meal; the equipment needs to be checked. They only spend an occasional night on the base now and then; the rest of the time they sleep in the safehouse they've set up in Sheberghan or camp by the roadside. 'Road' might be the wrong word here – in the four provinces that make up their area of responsibility there is only one main road that is paved, while the rest are pitted gravel roads or tire tracks in the sand. Or even just sand. It's dry and dusty in the summer, a mucky slush when it rains, and partly impassable in the winter.

I've come here to form an idea of what awaits Sweden if we someday assume leadership of the international military presence in this corner of the country, and to see what everyday life is like for our Swedish soldiers. Currently the British lead the military PRT that is responsible for four provinces in the north: Balkh, Jowzjan, Sar-e Pol and Samangan, and Sweden has less than a hundred people here under British command. But the plan is for Sweden to take over after Great Britain. PRT stands for Provincial Reconstruction Team, but these military units don't actually deal with reconstruction. Rather the intention is that the military presence will make the situation stable enough for the aid organizations to work here, and they are the ones who are to take care of reconstruction. Or construction, since there isn't much to reconstruct.

We eat heavy British food for dinner, then I spend most of the time talking to the Swedes who are puttering around the base, asking a hundred questions about what they do, and what they think about their jobs and their mission. The evening ends with an animated film, then I retire. I have been given my own section of a large guest tent. There are no other visitors here, at least no female visitors. I snap the tent shut, unroll my sleeping bag onto the cot, and fall asleep at once. I've spent twelve months of my life on a foreign mission, six of which entailed sleeping on this kind of narrow cot. The present moment feels like an agreeable flashback. This kind of life is so simple and so hard at the same time. Simple because the framework is fixed and no one would dream of changing it, hard because there is nowhere to hide and there's no freedom. And then there's the work on top of that, with everything that it can entail, from minutes of extreme stress to months of unbearable boredom.

In the morning, we set out toward the west. The team has two soft skin Toyota Land Cruisers – in other words, regular unarmored cars. We are three people in one car, four in the other. We listen to Johnny Cash, talk about this and that, and observe the landscape as we pass through. From time to time we stop, and Kim disappears along with Erik, the temporary squadron leader. They go and talk to the village elders and the local potentates, asking about the status and the security situation. But for the most part, the Afghans want to talk about all the things they lack: wells, schools, clinics, roads, and jobs. They sigh and point out that they already talked about all their troubles last year, and the year before, to Kim's and Erik's predecessors, but still nothing has happened. The road is still broken, the wells still not dug.

We arrive at Sheberghan, in Jowzjan Province, by dinnertime. The team's base there consists of a simple concrete building with camp beds in the rooms. The men take turns keeping watch and preparing meals using whatever ingredients they can get hold of – freshly prepared food provides a much-appreciated break here from the few standard meals that are available to choose from in the Armed Forces ration boxes, and all the instant coffee and dry crackers on the road.

Captain Kim has set up a punching bag in the yard, and soon he disappears outside dressed in workout clothes.

"You can accomplish a lot with a jumprope and an elastic band," he says. "You have to do what you can to stay in shape."

I remain sitting at the dining table; I don't feel like jumping rope right now. I jumped enough for a whole lifetime during recess in primary and elementary school. Instead, I drink tea out of a carved wooden cup and thumb through some old magazines that are lying on the faded oilcloth: *Café, Slitz, Runner's World*.

Sheberghan has no charm. It's a black hole where all joy disappears. Sheberghan is also the hometown of the warlord General Dostum. His house is just a few blocks away, but he also has one in my neighborhood in Kabul.

General Dostum is the leader of the Afghan Uzbeks. During his decades of spreading death and terror across the land, changing sides has been his ideology. Dostum began his career as a soldier in the Afghan army under the communist Soviet-backed regime of the 1970s, and he received some of his military training in the Soviet Union. He spent the 1980s fighting the American and Pakistan backed Mujahedin, on the side of the communist central power. Three years after the Soviet Union's departure, when the regime was greatly weakened, he switched sides and contributed to its fall.

The fall of the Najibullah regime in 1992 was the starting point for the bloody civil war between different Mujahedin factions which would continue until the Taliban had taken control of almost the entire country. During the civil war, General Dostum was first allied with the Tajik leader Massoud against the Pashtun Gulbuddin Hekmatyar. In 1994, he switched to Hekmatyar's side, now in order to wage war against the regime that Burhanuddin Rabbani had formed, supported by Massoud.

When the Taliban came on the scene, Dostum switched sides again, and now fought with Rabbani against the Taliban. As time went by, one of his subordinates made an agreement with the Taliban to capture the warlord Ismail Khan from Herat and deliver him to the Taliban in exchange for control of the country's northern parts. When the Taliban didn't keep their promise, Dostum found it necessary to escape to Turkey. He later came back to form new alliances, this time with the Americans against the Taliban. And finally, in President Karzai's first government, Dostum was appointed Deputy Defense Minister.

We set out early in the morning. The men have packed everything. I only have to keep track of myself, and barely even that – Captain Kim makes me toast and fixes sandwiches too, he rolls up my sleeping bag, checks and re-checks that I'm feeling well and have everything I need. His concern for all of us has no bounds; he flies around like a whirlwind.

"Peder, have you called home? How are the wife and kids? Everything good?"

"Joel, how's your headache? I have Alvedon tablets if you need them."

"Richard, any progress with the antenna?"

We travel westward, toward Andkhoy, near the border of Turkmenistan. Now we also have an interpreter with us, a lanky man whom no one in the group likes and no one quite trusts.

"Obviously he's reporting to someone else too, whether he wants to or not. And it's clear that everyone we talk to knows that, and behaves accordingly."

But what to do? Three years after we began our military engagement here, the Armed Forces interpreter school still trains mainly Russian speaking interpreters. It will be 2009 before the first group of Dari interpreters graduate and are ready for service.

After Andkhoy we turn north, straight into the desert, toward Turkmenistan. There are no longer any roads, only tire tracks in the desert sand, traces of trucks that we follow. We are traveling in order to find out if there is any control of the border at all.

The hours go by. We talk and listen to music. I force myself to think about other things besides landmines. If we're going to be blown up, I can accept that – if only it happens fast. But not the kind of drawn-out suffering and death agony that Johnny Cash sings about in his cover of *Mercy Seat* that we're listening to, over and over. We talk some more. I console myself with the fact that cars have driven here in the sand before – after all, I can see the tracks.

I will never understand the Swedish debate about our military effort in Afghanistan, or the politicians, pundits, and top military officers who call for thicker armor, more protection, and bigger vehicles. The idea of making a war not dangerous for the soldiers has its unique twisted logic. Of course it's dangerous. Why would we spend a 120 million dollars per year to send soldiers to places that aren't dangerous? This is no scout exercise, this is real. But when "force protection", or protecting one's own troops, becomes the main goal, then we might as well stay at home and hope that the danger won't reach us. We might as well pretend that we can isolate ourselves from the rest of the world. If we're unwilling to take certain calculated risks, we shouldn't be here in the first place.

The men are patient, pleasant, sweet; they see possibilities even in the sea of hopelessness. They have come here because they want to do something, and if anything, they are frustrated about the fact that they can't do more – that they aren't allowed to do more. I don't detect any nervousness about the risks that exist here – however distant they may seem to be today, here and now, as the sun warms the soft sand in all directions. The debate at home seems completely out of step with reality, misdirected in all its good intentions. If there's anything they wish for, it's to not have to pay tax on the instant coffee they drink by the roadside, not being able to lock themselves in on the base.

In the middle of nowhere we meet an eagle hunter. We stop the cars, and go out to talk to him and stretch our legs. He has an eagle in a rope to attract his prey. I force myself to look away from the eagle's eyes, which have been sewn shut. I want to drive on, not have to see.

Ah, finally the border. Two or three containers in various stages of disintegration have been deposited in the sand and serve as a border checkpoint. To either side, there is only emptiness. I can see for kilometers in each direction, and there's nothing but a few utility poles in the ground. This is the borderless society, long before Schengen: it's just a matter of driving, under cover of darkness, dust, or a suitable little sum of money.

We talk to the border police who are posted there. They lack communication equipment and the ability to patrol. They lack water. They lack everything. They seem happy to see us, and explain that they need higher pay and a few cars, maybe a pair of binoculars too. How do they get here? Get away from here? It's impossible to understand. We ask about smuggling, about the security situation, about what it is that's being transported across the border in the trucks whose tracks we have been following.

The last cup of tea has been drunk. We thank the men and drive a few more kilometers along the unpatrolled border before turning back to the south again. We want to get back to Andkhoy before dark.

We get a few kilometers further before the electrical system in one of the cars suddenly shuts down. Everything goes black, but the car still runs. We stop, look for a blown fuse, don't find anything, and decide to continue driving. It's already starting to get dark and soon it will be pitch-black, the way it gets in the desert at night.

I sit in the back seat of the car without electricity. We are driving diagonally behind the other car, feeling our way forward in the outer edge of its headlights. We weren't moving fast before, and now we're moving so slowly that it feels like we aren't getting anywhere at all.

It's late when we arrive. We drive through Andkhoy, which is dark except for a lamp on a wall here and there, and set up camp behind the ruins of some houses at the other edge of the city, close to the road. The men quickly pitch the tent by the light of their headlamps. It is very, very cold. They set up a night watch schedule and collect a few stones to throw at stray dogs if they get too close. They don't want to have to shoot them. I can just go and sleep. Before I know it, Kim has pumped up my air mattress for me and unrolled the sleeping bags.

I get a lesson on how to stay warm: mittens, hat, double sleeping bags, long underwear, rag socks. And a warm water bottle that Kim has prepared on top of that. I feel as pampered as a princess as I snuggle in to my bag.

When I wake up, there's frost on the inside of the tent. I lie there shivering for a little while before I can bring myself to crawl out of my cocoon. We pack up the night's camp and prepare to leave. The car with the electrical problem won't start at all today. The towlines are found, and now we have something that looks like a road back to Mazar-e Sharif and the base, but it will be slow going to tow the car all the way. Kim talks to headquarters about sending a tow truck to meet us somewhere along the way.

Hours go by as we drive at a snail's pace along the bumpy road. A few miles outside Mazar-e Sharif, the car they've sent finally comes, a big truck accompanied by a small army of staff officers who have taken the opportunity to go out on an excursion. A little bit like in the Scouts.

Now the only remaining problem is how we're going to get the car up onto the truck bed; no one had thought of that. And no one thought about where those of us who were riding in the car are going to sit now. Kim and his men exchange looks behind the backs of our rescuers, who scratch their heads and wonder what their plan was when they set out – if they had one at all.

Everyday Life [December 2004]

After months on the waiting list, I've managed to become a member of the gym at ISAF headquarters. The fortified base is in the center of the city, between the American embassy and the palace region.

Most of the people at the gym are German soldiers wearing t-shirts with tough slogans like *Wir machen Hausbesuche* ("We Make Housecalls") and a picture of German soldiers storming an Afghan house, brandishing automatic weapons. No, it isn't ironic; rather it's meant to impress someone back home, a token of manliness. I find it embarrassing more than anything else, especially since the Germans have so many restrictions on their participation in ISAF that they can barely even leave the base, let alone participate in any skirmishes. Embarrassing and painful. And undiplomatic as well... But I don't allow myself the luxury of being picky. A gym in Kabul is, in spite of everything, a gym in Kabul. I run on my treadmill as I watch them pump their biceps and triceps, which are already enormous, while their legs stick out from under their shorts like pale reeds. I stare at them, they stare at me – I'm sure our thoughts are not the same. It is unglamorous, but at least I get to sweat.

Sometimes I go to the home of Lasse and Matti, two men who work for Danish Demining Group, a Danish organization that clears landmines and ammunition. Matti has set up a training area in one of the outhouses, with mats, weights, and a punching bag. Matti looks like a cross between a weightlifter and a member of the motorcycle club Bandidos. In fact, he is a nurse with a kind heart and the patience of an angel.

Matti is training me in *krav maga*, an Israeli form of martial art, giving his instructions in the most beautiful Finland-Swedish accent I've ever heard. It's liberating to be able to punch, punch, punch until I can barely breathe. I pummel all of the week's failed compromises, persuasion, and discretion out of my system with as much power as I can muster. When I finish, I feel sore but happy as a pup.

At the Bottom of the Bottom of the World [December 2004/January 2005]

December 2004. A short visit to my home in a gray and overcast Stockholm, a place that soon seems the most foreign of all, with its red Christmas wrapping paper and gold ribbon and ham sandwiches. I suddenly can't interpret anything that's going around me. Everything solid evaporates. After more than four years, the only thing I've held on to, the only fixed point in my existence, is wiped out in the space of a few days in my own private tsunami.

It's strange how life changes from one day to the next. Sometimes it happens gradually, almost imperceptibly. Sometimes it happens in abrupt shifts, so abrupt that it's impossible to grasp the extent of what happened. A few words, and nothing will ever be the same as before.

"Everything is just broken," he says. "You feel so distant," he says. "We want such different things," he says.

After one more positional fight, everything is dead. I look around in the apartment that used to be ours. The flowers have withered, the milk soured, the dust bunnies sought shelter somewhere else. I look at him as he sits on the sofa, smoking. Painfully I remember the day when I fell hopelessly in love with him. Now time has finally managed to peel away this love, the way you peel an onion. Layer after layer after layer, until there's nothing left but tears.
  "Why did you have to go to Kabul?"
  I wanted to do my job, for whatever that's worth. I didn't want to get stuck in a web of non-essentials.
  "Why do I have to be here? Why do you have to be here?"
  Who says life has to happen in Stockholm? Why is your reality more important than mine?

I return to Kabul with a tangled-up brain and a pitch-black empty space carved out of my heart. I arrive at my house, surrounded by Chinese whorehouses and flocks of ragged children carrying shoeshine boxes on their shoulders. From the garden, I hear the monotonous humming of the generator, like a requiem for what used to be. A hymn to failure. A few flies who have survived the winter keep me company through the stew of crushed dreams that is the only thing left. With a sliver of glass in my heart and another in my stomach, I lie in bed. Broken. Distant. With a will of my own.

If the soul exists, it must be located in the stomach; that's where you feel things. That's the spot where the air doesn't reach no matter how much I breathe. Who am I to blame him? Sometimes I can barely stand to live with myself: destructive as an armored battalion, hard, and unwilling to compromise.

All I want to do is fall apart. I fall apart. I lie on my bed under a pile of blankets, fully dressed, with my teeth chattering. I wait for the liberating amnesia of insanity to appear. I decide to give up. Someone will have to take me away from here. Give me therapy. Care. Medicine. Amputate my soul, my stomach, my head, or wherever all the feelings that hurt so much are located. Take away everything to be on the safe side. Just cut it out, no need for any anesthesia.

Once I've let myself fall apart, I realize that it doesn't make any difference. There's no help to be had. It's just me here, alone in a frozen house at the bottom of the bottom of the world. I might as well go down to the kitchen and make myself a cup of tea. Eat up the leftover Christmas candy. Maybe call up Nick and ask if he wants to swing by the Elbow Room.

Days go by. Weeks go by. I keep my head above water. I'm thankful that I'm not in Stockholm, that I'm not looking for him among the people on the streets. This, what's here, this is only mine. Let him walk around over there in uptight, predictable Stockholm, with its January slush, as much as he wants to. Kabul has never been more important. I go to work seven days a week, thankful for the darkness and the desolation, for the unlit street lights and the empty streets. I'm thankful that I have a job that can occupy all of my waking hours. Something real and important to escape to while my soul's protective shell is growing back. A reality that sometimes helps give me distance to my paltry problems. I have food on the table (a little monotonous with all that rice, but at least it's food), a roof over my head (frozen, but the snow can't get in), family and friends alive and well (even if they are a continent away). Who am I to complain?

Kandahar [February 2005]

It's early February when we leave Kabul, a winter more bitter than anyone can remember. The olive oil on my kitchen counter has frozen. On the street outside the house, children dressed in cotton shirts and plastic sandals without socks play in the snow that never stops falling. They build snowmen as their hands become chapped and their red noses run. I try to see if anyone is missing from yesterday, if anyone has frozen to death during the night. But there are so many of them, all these children – the children who are carrying other children, the children who are wandering around in the neighborhood without schooling to think about or real shoes on their feet.

A cracked scab of ice covers the road toward Kandahar. The landscape is blanketed in snow, barren and cold, the most inhospitable place there could be. A whole country against the wind.

We stop for a rest in Qarabagh. On the map it's marked as a town, but it hardly qualifies. Outside the butcher shop, a few animal carcasses are hanging from the roof. On the ground, a horse's head lies in the snow, which looks like currant sorbet. We visit the town's *chai khana*. The teahouse doesn't have a separate room for women, but we are allowed into the room anyway, which is empty and without furniture. We settle down on the floor and are given a kettle and some glasses. The tea leaves dance in the steaming water. Within a few minutes the room is filled with men and young boys in turbans made of enormous pieces of cloth. Some of them seem to have an entire laundry basket carefully wound around their crowns. One man has his Kalashnikov with him. As the English traveler Robert Byron writes in his book *The Road to Oxiana* from 1937, Afghans carry their weapons as naturally as a British man carries his umbrella. No one has described it better.

The men line up soundlessly along the walls to stare at the *kafirs*, or unbelievers, on the floor. They just stare. A silence as solid and dense as mud rests over the place. The only occasional sound is from a bird sitting in a far too small cage. I sip my green tea with its taste of hay. I adjust my scarf, which never wants to stay in place around my head. I tug and tug at my sweater and regret that I didn't put on a longer jacket, something more suitable. I stir the tea in the chipped glass on the floor in front of me. I feel like the main act in an annual stalker convention. I've never felt myself watched so intently.

We pay and drive on. The road is covered in snow; everything is draped in white. There's nothing but snow everywhere. The towns and villages we pass through have no electricity; only the utility poles are left. They seem to have no women either. During the whole trip, I never see a single woman, and only occasionally a shabbily dressed man, plodding along by the side of the road in a fruitless struggle against the pitiless elements. Otherwise the landscape is as deserted as if a neutron bomb had hit.

Somewhere on the road through the Zabul province we stop for a smoking break. The sky is steel gray and a cold wind cuts across the landscape. As I stand by the roadside and look out over the province, I can see my breath in the cold air, and I feel more keenly alive than I have in a long time. It doesn't get more dangerous than this. But the white-drenched landscape is peaceful. It reminds me of a foggy December morning somewhere in the middle of Sweden, one of those days when the sun can't quite manage to shine.

After eight hours we reach Kandahar, a little piece of the Middle Ages in the year 2005. There's no snow, but the rain is pouring down. It's the first rain in eight years, people tell us.

This is the Taliban heartland. This is the Taliban world, where the promised future exists in the past. It was here in Kandahar that the movement emerged in 1994. Then, as now, it was a revolt against the central power and its inability to delivery security. The country was close to disintegrating. The Soviet retreat and later, the fall of the Soviet-supported communist PDPA (People's

Democratic Party of Afghanistan) regime, did not lead to peace, but rather to a bloody civil war between different factions of Mujahedin, the Afghan rebels who had fought against the Russians. Competing warlords each ruled over their own little regions, where they plundered, raped, and kidnapped the population as they wished. When the village mullah Mohammed Omar, along with a few other students from the madrasa, or Islamic school, was able to challenge a warlord, he quickly gained popularity. The supporters around him soon swelled into a small army, and the Taliban movement was born. Wherever it went, law and order was established – even if it was by brutal means. Two years later it controlled most of the country.

Many Afghans now look back on the Taliban era with nostalgia, as a time of relative security and stability. When it first ended people had so many hopes, as the eyes of the world suddenly turned toward the country after decades of suffering. Now it was finally over. Now it would finally get better. The refugees could return home from neighboring countries, families' wounds could heal. Finally, people would be able to look ahead, toward jobs and a daily life free from terror. But the high and unrealistic expectations placed on the new administration and the support of the world powers have not been fulfilled. And how could they have been? It is slow and difficult to build a state, but courage and hope, fragile after so many setbacks, are quickly lost. The disappointment over President Hamid Karzai's administration should not be underestimated. The administration is weak and divided into factions, and it becomes more corrupt every month. The security situation is gradually worsening. The president has not succeeded in challenging the much despised warlords from the days of the civil war, if indeed he ever had any intention of doing so. Instead, they have been shuffled around between different posts as police chiefs, ministers, and governors, where they continue to hold the dark memories alive. The new national police force is notoriously corrupt and still, after many years of effort, they contribute to Afghanistan's security problems more than they help to solve them. The Afghan army is more highly regarded, but is poorly equipped and spread too thin.

When we arrive at the place where we plan to spend the night, it is already dark. A man at the UN guesthouse receives us. He shows us to our rooms in the chilly house. Mine is about as cozy as an operating room: four bare walls, a lopsided plywood cupboard, and a bed with sheets that smell like a gym bag. The pool of light from the lamp forms a perfect ring on the depressing carpet. I make myself a nest under the pilled blanket before falling into a restless sleep.

We meet with Governor Gul Agha Sherzai. When he enters the room, it feels as if a wind of cold air blows through it. He is a warlord with a meaty face and lips like little sausages pressed together. It's empty and cold, and the curtains in his swanky, newly built four million dollar residence remind me of the ones I've seen in Russia. We drink green tea and eat nuts.

"You should stay here," Gul Agha scolds us.

"Thank you, that's very gracious, but we are staying at the UN guesthouse. We've already checked in," Ann defends herself. She is my boss, who has come here from Islamabad.

"But why aren't you staying here?"

Gul Agha looks sharply at us and waves toward the desolate, inhospitable house. He is a man who is not used to being questioned.

"You are *my* guests," he complains, like a sulky, insufferable child.

We shift our weight uncomfortably as we sit on the edge of the ghastly couches. But at last he gives up and changes the subject. We hear about how problem-free everything is in the province, how human rights are respected. We hear about how there is order and stability nowadays.

"The situation is normal. Everything is under control," he says with a sharp tone.

The lies come as naturally as breath to him.

"Everything is in the process of normalizing," he insists.

He sounds like a worn out barrel-organ, but the high, effective wall of denial he's erected around himself makes it hard for the words to reach. He tells us about his plans for the province. Development is going forward, he says. A park is being built where people can stroll on Fridays. Everything is normal. A slightly surreal sensation mixes with the air in the room. The new furniture gleams, the couches creak. Gul Agha takes a swig of his tea, sweetened with self-satisfaction, and drones on. Ann is silent. I can't think of anything suitable to say either. Here, truth is an unknown concept, a verbal, empty magic trick.

The meeting is over. We may go. When I reach out my hand for a parting handshake, he takes it reluctantly. His grip could crush bones.

The next day, we meet the American leader of the war against terrorism in this part of the country. Behind walls made of Hesco bastion and barbed wire lies the American camp, a pocket of USA in this great desert-covered province in the middle of Central Asia. An enclave of grounded outlets, tough paper napkins, brownies, hiphop music, and rules that are followed.

A young soldier equipped with an automatic weapon, pistol, helmet with protective glasses, knife, radio, bulletproof vest, watch with compass, and military harness stops us at the gate. He looks almost baroque in his excess.

"Yes, ma'am?" he says with a drawling accent.

"We have a meeting with the commander," says Ann.

The soldier looks at us suspiciously.

"I am the Swedish ambassador," she adds with a sigh.

The man goes away. He moves like a tin soldier. Clump, clump, clump. After a brief conversation in a field telephone that looks like it could probably survive a direct hit from a Scud missile, he reluctantly lets us in.

The friendly colonel has a crew cut and walks with a rhythmic gait. He offers us American brewed coffee and delivers a briefing filled with smart one-liners, arrows, maps, and Powerpoint slides. Maximum content with a minimum number of words; black and white. Maybe the rain outside has washed away all of Afghanistan's dingy gray nuances. I leave the briefing soothed by an odd feeling that the world is simple, understandable, and manageable. Who has the energy to care about the catalog of mistakes, the senseless killing, and all the official lies that are the basic elements of every war? Not me, at least not right now.

The colonel's assistant leads us to the tax-free shop on the base. As if bewitched, I walk around in the airy space, touching jam jars and wool socks. Ann looks at a bomber jacket with the words "Operation Enduring Freedom" printed on the back, unsure if it's supposed to be for the ironic generation or simply taken at face value. Operation Enduring Freedom. I reflect that the American spin doctors who came up with that name didn't have the prisoners in Guantánamo in mind. No one thinks about them. They are terrorists, the global excuse for almost anything at all, a carte blanche for a series of wrongs. *In order to fight evil one has to fight humanity.*

I can't help but wonder what exactly goes on at the gigantic base. While I'm walking around here stocking up on Oreo cookies, aspirin, and warm socks of the best quality, maybe some suspected al-Qaeda activist or Taliban leader is being brought here, before being sent on to the network of secret prisons and interrogation centers that the CIA are reputed to have all over the world, for prisoners who are taken from one underground world to another.

Darkness falls, and we are back at the UN guesthouse. My excitement after all the new impressions from the day is gone, and I feel that all my enthusiasm has run out. I'm exhausted from all the conversations, from everything I'm trying to understand, from all the questions without answers. Sitting on the bed in my room, I try to keep my thoughts in check with a little paperwork. Useless. I try to call someone, but can only reach a mechanical voice that tells me it's impossible to make a connection. Today it isn't possible to call from one world to another. I just feel so far away. I look around the small shabby room and wonder how I'll ever be able to sleep.

A few days later, we drive to the Maiwand District in the pattering rain. I'm sitting in the back seat, looking out over the barren landscape and listening to the sound of the windshield wipers flinging themselves across the windshield. There's nowhere I'd rather be. This is what I love most of all – being on the road.

The road soon turns into tire tracks, the tire tracks soon turn into mud. Dusk falls. The police escort vehicle that the governor has sent with us gets stuck in the mud near the grave of the national heroine Malalai, out on a windswept field.

"This will become heroin," says Ustad Haqmar, the village elder from Maiwand who has come with us as a guide.

He points to the innocent little green poppy plants at the side of the road and tugs thoughtfully at his white Santa Claus beard. To my untrained eye, the field looks like a strawberry field.

"We have to get back to the guesthouse before dark," says Kabir, our driver, with a tight voice.

He nods toward the armed escorts who have spread out around the cars.

"There are only sixteen of them."

The words are left hanging in the darkening evening air.

The thin soldiers look searchingly toward the mountains at the horizon and grip their Kalashnikovs, decorated with tape in happy colors. How long could they hold them off, I wonder. I don't know; I'm no military strategist. But it was somewhere around here that the British suffered one of their most serious defeats ever in Asia, during the Second Anglo-Afghan War in the summer of 1880. The British brigadier general George Burrows misjudged his opponent Ayub Khan and clashed with his forces. The British were outnumbered and exhausted from the heat, but did their best, in fighting that was often man-to-man. In *The Great Game. The Struggle for Empire in Central Asia*, the British historian Peter Hopkirk describes how the soldiers, with a steady grip on the Afghans' beards, speared them on their British bayonets and threw stones at them to keep them at bay, as they ran out of ammunition. When the day was over and the remaining troops retreated to Kandahar, the British had lost close to a thousand men.

As Kabir winches up the escort car from the mud, our host points out a house on the mountain slope a few kilometers away.

"Look over there – one of Osama bin Laden's houses."

A new day. We set out at dawn to drive to the neighboring province, Helmand. For a few hours we drive westward along the country road to Gereshk, before turning off to the south on a miserable gravel road.

A few more hours, and we find ourselves on the next level in the cone of hell. In Lashgar Gah, the capital of the province, we meet a man rumored to be one of Afghanistan's uncrowned drug kings – the governor himself. Sher Mohammed meets us with film cameras and an unlikely group of local potentates. They are all men. Sher Mohammed is a thin man with a checkered turban. It looks like he's wearing a swaying soft ice cream cone on his head. His eyes have a glint of insanity and an unbridled ruthlessness that makes me shudder.

The governor invites us to lunch. We sit down at the long table, laden with kebab on skewers, rice, fruit, and bread. Men with movie cameras stumble around behind the chairs, documenting every bite. It's almost impossible for anyone but Sher Mohammed to get a word in edgewise. All through lunch, he holds forth about all the various aid projects he and his people wish for – no, demand: Bridges, roads, schools, clinics. He complains about the unrealized projects, the ones that the international community promised.

Yes, we have promised a lot. But most of the residents of Helmand have received nothing, except for fleas and parasites and the cold of the winter outside the door. It's an everyday reality that squeezes the life spirit out of people like dirty water out of a dishrag.

"Why have you come here?" asks a young man with a filling of baby fat under his smooth skin, as we rise from the table.
I hesitate. Yes, why? Because. *Like a beetle trapped in amber.*

After lunch, we visit the city jail. It looks essentially like an ordinary mud brick house, without heat, water, or electricity. The prisoners, some of them maybe no more than 15 years old, are standing in clusters, looking at us. They stare unremittingly. A Chopinesque feeling of melancholy takes hold of me as I look out over this real-life vale of tears. I haven't seen this much despair concentrated in one place since I visited a refugee camp in Ingushetia, where the Chechen refugees had been living in barns for years. I stand there with my new shoes sunk into the mud, speechless. And there, sadly, I finally see some women. There are three of them. They have all been sentenced to years behind the mud walls for "moral crimes", the code for unfaithfulness or the offense of being seen with a man who is not a relative. But I never find out whether this unfaithfulness was even voluntary. They might have been raped.

The women sit hunched under their shawls, mute and with eyes that are already dead. One looks so brittle that she seems two-dimensional; her face is wrinkled up like a piece of paper and her skin hangs like thin fabric around her wrists. A living corpse, a person with hell both behind and ahead of her.

I hold my notebook in front of me like a shield against all the heartbreak. I carefully write down the things that are told to me on the lined pages. As if it made any difference. As if the details were important. As if my government-issued composition book could provide these women restitution, or give the prisoners their life back. If I had been able to speak then, I would have wanted to say I'm sorry. I'm sorry that our policies are not enough. I'm sorry that we can't do more. Instead I nod mutely, smile the friendliest smile I have. Smile and swallow my pain.

It's still raining on our last day. Before continuing on our journey to the Pakistan border, we spend an hour looking around the city of Kandahar. We drive to the mosque where Mullah Omar used to go to pray. We don't go to Zor Shahr, the old city. "Check with the UNAMA office and local Afghans about possible minefields before exploring this site," my UN-published handbook advises. *Over my dead body will I walk around in a minefield, cleared or not.* We visit the city's old 18th-century mosque, with the most beautiful walls in ochre red and blue. Wherever we go, a group of children and adults gather, in plastic sandals or barefoot; they gather around us and just stare. Look here, an exotic theater troupe from the West!

"Look! Women!" I hear myself say as the car rolls out through the city. I can hardly recognize my own voice.

I point to two women dressed in burkas among the throngs of people.

"It's Friday and a holiday" Kabir explains.

It doesn't matter what he says. It doesn't matter what anyone says. I will never, ever understand this country.

A One-Way Ticket to Quetta
[February 2005]

Spin Boldak. It is an almost impossibly beautiful name for this spot along the porous Afghanistan-Pakistan border. A broken road. Flags that struggle in the icy wind. Muddy slush. A few kiosks selling car parts. Not a single Coca-Cola sign with false promises about a happier world, a sated future.

It's the middle of February. The air is as harsh as the damp wool of a hand-knitted mitten, and a sun that gives off no warmth at all mocks us from the eternally blue sky. My boss Ann, my colleague Dag, and I stand shivering and bargaining with a taxi driver to take us to Quetta, in Balochistan, on the other side of the border. We spend half an hour chasing down someone who can stamp our passports on the Afghan side, and finally find him in a mosque. Then the taxi sets off. With us are two freeriders from the village, who hang on to the back of the minibus.

We pass the Pakistan border unchallenged.

"That's my cousin," the driver explains with a nod toward the uniformed border guard he just embraced. He shifts gears.

Yes, why not? The border is nothing more than a line on a map, drawn by an Englishman without regard to ethnic or topographical factors. It runs through tribes, through villages, and divides Pashtuns on one side from Pashtuns on the other. Until now I haven't met a single Pashtun who acknowledges it.

After ten minutes, the driver stops. One of the two freeriders leans in through the window. He stretches his frozen hands toward the little fan with its tired stream of warm air. He wants to get in.

"This is my brother. My brother!" entreats the driver, pulling him by the sleeve. His eyes are like lapis lazuli, intensely blue, hard, and cold.

"We're sorry."

We shake our heads. No, we don't feel like riding in a taxi with more strange men. The brother sighs, breathes on his fists to warm them, and climbs onto the back of the minibus again. I have a terrible guilty feeling. It's only a few degrees outside, and after a winter in Afghanistan I know what it means to be cold, to go through the day with your very soul wrapped in frost.

We go at a roaring pace along the winding roads toward Quetta. In spite of the uphill road and limited view, our driver forces the taxi past overloaded buses and trucks painted with flowers. The asphalt glitters with frost. From the cracked speakers of the car's tape player, unintelligible words seep out, set to Balochi pop. I'm thrown now forward, now backward in my seat. I force my gaze away from the road, fix it on the landscape. Tinder-dry mountains rise up against the azure blue sky, decorated with fluffy clouds. Tinder-dry ravines throw themselves headlong down the slopes. We pass a caravan of *Kutji*, or nomads. Girls in brightly colored clothes and shawls sit on top of the camels' matted backs; the camel calves walk with thin, tired legs. The lined faces of the men rush by along the roadside. In a valley, a piece of railway meanders like a fragmentary, fleeting dream of modernity.

The journey goes on, the hours crawl by. Dusk falls. Suddenly the driver brakes.
"We have to stop. It's prayer time."
He finds a shawl and steps out of the car. The freeriders jump off and make a fruitless attempt to brush the travel dust from their clothes. The two wretches are covered in dirt and have wrapped their shawls around their heads, leaving only two narrow slits for their eyes. They look like they've stepped out of a BBC report on Hamas. We're standing on the outskirts of a miserable village. An architectural design year would do this place good, a little electricity even more. Poverty, ugliness – the polar opposite of the highly aestheticized existence in Stockholm that I left behind, in what already feels like an eternity ago, another life.

What was the creator thinking when he put people here in the middle of nowhere? Was he thinking at all? Because it must have been a he – no woman would be so damned unpractical and cruel. I can see the men, and their public display of religion, through the dirty window. Up and down. Down and up. *Al-islam huwa al-hall.* Islam is the solution – to the economic and political problems, the social injustices. But since the Islamic Republic of Pakistan was founded in 1947, the idea of using Islamic laws and principles to solve economic problems or social injustice, to take on corruption, hypocrisy, or nepotism, hasn't worked very well. It's so much simpler to concentrate on the women and make sure that they are kept in check, in the name of God, the Most Gracious, the Most Merciful. Throughout the ages, people have been oppressed in the name of religion. As long as religion is considered to be above critical discussion, what better weapon could there be?

I'm dogged by renewed feelings of shame as the driver eases out on the road again. The supposed brother just barely manages to hang on to the bus before we head into the dust.

It's dark when we approach Quetta. The Balochi pop cassette is playing for the fourth time through, and I'm starting to recognize the songs. One more prayer break and we are there. The five-star hotel Serena glitters in the dark, like a mirage after a week on the road. It's like falling in through the gates of heaven. I never, never, never want to go home to my frozen house in Kabul again.

The next day our program begins early. Breakfast with nationalists, meetings with nationalists, lunch with nationalists, more meetings with nationalists. Finally, a dinner with nationalists. Frustration, powerlessness, hatred, and bloodthirstiness come out in gasps between bites of rice, chicken, and pizza. They complain about social tensions, political corruption, and economic misery. They tell us about the abuses and injustices of the Punjab-dominated central power, and about their own training camps and weapon deliveries. The words are fired like cartridges from a gun. Baloch or Pashtun – it makes no difference; they all willingly throw fuel on the fire to keep the brew of discontent, separatism, and extremism simmering. What is myth, and what is truth? What is only an attempt to secure a political future? I will never find out. I sit there with my notebook and pen, but can't manage to write anything down on the lined paper. All my new insights into the miserable state of the world and my own narrow-mindedness have paralyzed the communications between my head and my hand.

Back again in my hotel room, I look around me with foreign eyes: here is a backdrop of excess right in the epicenter of the Pakistani misery. I think about the long line of random life events that have led me precisely here, to a foreign land, until I fall asleep among the down comforters.

The next morning, we venture out for a bit of Taliban tourism. Our guide, a clearsighted and crass journalist, shuttles us away from the main streets of the old British garrison town with its handsome facades, whitewashed walls, and swarms of mustachioed paramilitary. We drive to the neighborhood of Pashtunabad. Soon the car can barely make its way through the misery among the houses.

"This is where the Taliban plan and steer their infiltration activities in the southern parts of Afghanistan," our friend says.

"Only Taliban live here, and they're left alone."

Yes, that makes sense. The Taliban are not without supporters, and they didn't come out of nowhere. And the Taliban's view of women is nothing that raises people's eyebrows on this side of the border. Pakistan is not so much a patriarchy as a society saturated with an undisguised hatred of women. Here too women are property, like any other kind of property, like a donkey, or a shoe, or a Tupperware jug. It is not unusual that when a husband passes away, the wife is included in the inheritance – she's married off to the brother or one of his other relatives. But only rarely do any of the problems of the Pakistani women make waves in international news.

One exception is the case of Mukhtar Mai. In June of 2002, Mukhtar Mai was raped in her home village Meerwala, in southern Punjab, by order of the village council. The reason was that her twelve-year-old brother, Shakoor, was accused of having been seen in the company of a woman from the Mastoi clan, and the brother had thereby sullied the honor of that clan. Shakoor's family claimed that the accusations were fabricated and that Shakoor had in fact been sexually exploited by men from the Mastoi clan.

So Shakoor was arrested by police for adulterous relations. The village council was called and decided that Shakoor was to marry the woman he had shamed, and that Mukhtar Mai would simultaneously be married to a man from the Mastoi clan. But the Mastoi clan refused, and Mukhtar Mai was called to the council to apologize for her brother's behavior. When she came, she was dragged to a nearby shed and raped by four men, whereupon the Mastoi clan told police that the problem was solved. And Shakoor was released by the police.

There the story should have ended: one woman's fate, similar to thousands of others. But Mukhtar Mai summoned up her courage and spoke out, and her fate came to be publicized to the world.

The uproar from the international press and international organizations was followed by arrests and releases, and arrests and releases and appeals, until the case reached the highest court. At that point only one of the six was still in custody. Of course there was also Mukhtar Mai, who feared for her life. Her passport was confiscated, and she ended up on the Pakistani state's official list of people who are forbidden to leave the country, because she had dishonored Pakistan's reputation.

This is justice in the upside-down world. This, I assume, is the famous respect for "their" women that so many Afghan and Pakistani men talk about when I meet them. They go on and on while I say nothing. I'm silent and I tell myself that I have to choose my battles; I'm smarter than Don Quixote.

The car rolls on toward the next Taliban den, the bottom of the car scrapes against yet another stone. I adjust my shawl for the hundredth time as we roll by some turban-clad men leading a donkey. They look like a hippie collective from the Middle Ages, with their *patloos*, or blankets, homemade clothes, and billowing beards.

"There's another safe haven for Taliban leaders," our guide says.

He nods toward a tin door as we slowly pass by.

We're quiet in the car. A boy with a black turban looks at me with amazement. He has the Koran pressed against his chest. Or maybe it's a schoolbook, the kind that teaches people how to wash their armpits in a particular Islamic way and other useful things. The Taliban flag waves from a shabby house. The stench of poverty is all around. Poverty can take so many different forms that there aren't enough words to describe it, nor enough imagination for the senses to picture it. This only looks like an ordinary kind of misery, nothing remarkable. But it's here among the ruins that young, angry men are transformed into human bombs – suicide bombers with messages that we are unable to interpret.

Winter

At my goodbye party before I traveled to Kabul, in an apartment on Heleneborgsgatan filled with people and the buzz of voices, I was given a book by Torsten Örn as a gift. *Why Diplomacy?* was the title. I've read it without finding any answer to that question. But sometimes I take it off the shelf and thumb through it. If I want to raise my blood pressure I flip to the page where Torsten himself, dressed in tails and a top hat, looks boldly out at me. The caption under the photo reads, "The everyday life of diplomacy, where parties are a workday routine". I wonder in which planetary system Torsten got to be a diplomat, which galaxy he represented. I look out through the living room window, past the few rosebushes covered in frost, and at the dirty wall. There's no need for a tailcoat over here, but it would be nice to have a beaver nylon overall, because it's so damned cold and I never stop feeling frozen.

Herat [February 2005]

It's a gray, cloudy, and cold day, and I'm sitting in the car on my way to the airport.

"You go to Herat, Miss Diana?"

Wahab's gaze meets mine in the rearview mirror. I nod. "Yes."

"They have electricity in Herat."

He pronounces the words carefully, as if they were fragile, as if it were a confidential secret that the rest of the world can't tolerate hearing.

"So I have heard."

"All the time."

"Mmm."

I share the Afghans' obsession with the power supply. Here you don't talk about the weather; you talk endlessly about the electric supply. When I come home, the first thing I ask my guards about is whether there's electricity. *How many hours did you have yesterday? None? You know, last week we had electricity all day Friday. All day! It didn't disappear until midnight. But in the neighboring block they haven't had any electricity at all in three weeks. Can you imagine?*

That's how we all carry on, with innumerable variations. An hour, two hours, a day, two weeks. Sometimes the current is so weak that the filament in the lightbulb is just barely visible in the dark; sometimes the surges are so strong that everything that's plugged in breaks. Everything valuable in my house – TV, computer, refrigerator – is connected to heavy, clumsy, Chinese-manufactured stabilizers, so that if there's a surge they will take the brunt of it – unless they also break.

Six percent of Afghanistan's energy needs are met. How can you get a country on its feet without electricity? What industry, what little workshop, what store can manage without electricity? What can you produce, or what services can you deliver, without electricity? During the dark part of the year when daylight only lasts a few hours, all human energy is spent keeping the cold at bay and the body warm and fed. Aside from opium, Afghanistan exports only nuts and hand-knotted rugs. How can you keep 25 million people fed and warm from that? (Or is it 35 million? No one knows.) You can't be effective or productive without electricity. It just doesn't work. You can hardly think. Descartes was right, thoughts can freeze.

To compensate, those who can afford it have some little diesel generator that bangs and lets out black exhaust fumes, in order to be able to turn on the lights in the dark shop if some customer happens to come along, or to be able to run the sewing machine for a while. The diesel is driven from Pakistan to Kabul by truck over the mountains – a long, long journey.

Anyway. Filled with expectation, I board the plane, eager to go and play with the electric switches over there for a few days.

Herat is the hometown of the Tajik Ismail Khan, and Herat's relative wellbeing is largely attributed to him. Ismail Khan looks quite a bit like Santa Claus, with his white beard and his rotund figure. Nonetheless, he's one of the better-known warlords and represents a conservative interpretation of Islam. When Ismail Khan was deposed from his post as provincial governor in September 2004, many people wanted to see this as a sign that the president finally intended to clean up among the warlords. However, these hopes were dashed last Christmas, when Khan was brought in from the cold directly into the newly formed government, where he was given a position as minister of energy.

I'm staying with my friend Sofie and her Canadian fiancé Garth. Sofie and I are both Swedes, but we have never seen each other in Sweden. I met her through a mutual friend when I was traveling in Baku. I was on vacation, while she was writing her dissertation about Islamic activism in Azerbaijan. It's as if globalization has swept over my circle of acquaintances; we move around the earth as easily as my grandparents moved around their home parish in Västerbotten, Sweden.
Now we're sitting in Garth's and Sofie's enormous house, drink-

ing tea and eating Iranian candies. We talk about life, about Islam, about Afghanistan, about her dissertation, about my work, and about whether microcredit is the key to battling poverty. We're sitting in the large sectional couch and I'm wishing we could move the office here instead, because I've fallen head over heels in love with the city. "Finally, an Asia without inferiority complex," writes the eccentric Robert Byron after arriving in Herat in 1933.

"Where does it come from?"

"What?" asks Sofie.

"The electricity."

"From Iran, like everything else here."

Herat has not only electricity, but also water, and a working telephone system and roads paved with asphalt. It's almost like coming to another country, a little bit of Iran that has infiltrated Afghanistan. The shops carry Iranian goods almost exclusively. Commerce is Herat's most important source of income. The province is the connection point for trade with Turkmenistan to the north and Iran to the west. Much more than half of Afghanistan's customs income supposedly comes from Herat, and Ismail Khan, during the years he has ruled this province, has been unwilling to send the money to Kabul. Instead it's gone into his own business, including his militia, but also to the city and its population.

The shops are full. The roads are paved. Trees line the streets – by contrast, in Kabul there's almost nothing green. All the trees were chopped down during the war, when people needed firewood and heat. I haven't seen so much as a stump. Everything has been used. But here, there are trees – dusty, thirsty, but trees nonetheless.

I spend a few days meeting journalists and representatives from the UN, local non-governmental organizations (NGOs), and political parties. And I meet Mark, a Brit who works for Ronco, an organization financed by the U.S. State Department whose mission is to render harmless the incredible munitions dumps that sit under the open sky in this province.

"I work with amazing people. And there's so much to do. We blow up tons of munitions every week: Soviet, American, Saudi, British, Egyptian, Chinese. And stocks of mines. There's everything here, and lots of it. You should come with me some day!"

He makes it sound as if they go out and pick mushrooms. One cache here in the glade, one over there. But nothing can make me go near a landmine that is about to be blown up. Not alive, anyway.

Mark tells me that one day, he asked everyone on the team to bring a burka to work. Once they were there, he urged all the men to work in the burka all day. They laughed and joked around, they took pictures of each other and worked – though it was almost impossible to get any work done when you could hardly see anything, or move without getting stuck in the cloth, or having the cloth getting stuck in something.

"After that, two of them went home and asked their wives to take off their burkas."

He shrugs his shoulders and tilts his head a little to one side.

"It's better than nothing."

When I ask around, people tell me that the air is easier to breathe nowadays. Many are hopeful. After Ismail Khan's dethroning, more women dare to go out on the streets, some of them dressed in *chador*, the black costume that doesn't cover the eyes, instead of burkas. News channels have reported on other things besides Ismail Khan's actions; even a film or two from the West gets shown. Journalists are taking a few more risks. A radio station for and by women has started broadcasting, and a gym for women has opened its doors. Herat takes me by surprise and fills me with optimism and belief in the future.

A year or so later, Fauzia Gailiani, the woman who opened the gym, would stop by my office in Kabul and talk about her work in the chaotic parliament. She won the place in *Wolesi Jirga*, or the House of the People, after a successful election campaign in which she ran against her former husband. She received more than 16,800 votes, making her one of the most popular of the 5,800 candidates who competed for the 249 places in the lower house and the seats in the 34 provincial councils. This successful, divorced Afghan mother of six, who teaches aerobics and sits in Parliament, sank down into one of the armchairs in my office. With a scarf around her head and a blouse revealing Madonna-like biceps, she complained about her backward parliamentary colleagues and the unruly sessions. It is conversations like this that keep me going for weeks, filled with purpose; conversations like this remind me that Afghanistan is so much more than the worn out clichés about it. There are as many facets of Afghanistan as there are grains of sand.

One afternoon, Sofie and Garth take me sightseeing. We go to a burka shop where I carefully choose one for myself, a blue one. We visit a little antique shop that sells handblown glass and all kinds of jewelry and other objects. We go to Masjid-e Jumah, the Friday Mosque. It's no less than a miracle that it's survived so well through the centuries of war and unrest. I'm awestruck by the beauty; with its arabesques, mosaics, and calligraphy in turquoise, blue, and green, this is the most beautiful thing that I've seen in Afghanistan. The mosaic glitters like the sea in the cold sun, and the stones are chilly against my sock-clad feet. The only other people there are a group of old men with white turbans and graying beards. They sit nearly motionless on an ochre-red carpet, talking softly, and I can hear the click of the prayer beads that run through their fingers. I envy them. I wish that I too could sit in stillness on the carpet, surrounded by this beauty, and just let the hours slip by, feeling myself at peace.

We finish our sightseeing with a visit to the 15th-century minarets that reach swaying up toward eternal bliss. Once, there were thirty minarets, and the high towers were covered in blue and green mosaic. The five that now remain are as brown as the desert around them, like factory chimneys dipped in cocoa, pockmarked by bullet holes and grenade shards. We stay sitting in the car, at the side of the two-lane road that goes through them, squinting up at them with our necks craned. The ground around the towers hasn't been demined; it is probably safe, but none of us want to take the risk.

"The minarets have survived the destruction of the country, but now traffic is their biggest threat," Sofie says laconically.

Yes: maybe one of the last cultural treasures of Afghanistan will finally fall apart from the vibrations of some passing truck on its way to Iran to pick up pastries.

The next day I ride the few miles to Islam-Qalah at the Iranian border, together with some representatives from UNHCR, the UN refugee agency. It was only a few months ago that the newly rebuilt road was unveiled by President Karzai and Iran's President Khatami. It's a perfectly asphalted highway through the desolate, barren landscape, with a road sign or two along the way. A gift from the influential neighbor in the west to his poor cousin – a tribute to the relationship, so heartfelt on paper, between Iran and Afghanistan.

The Tajiks in Afghanistan are of Iranian origin and speak Persian, but I have trouble seeing any kind of brotherly love between the two peoples. Throughout its history, the relationship between the neighbor countries has never been uncomplicated or particularly warm. After his implausible journey through Persia and Afghanistan and back again, Byron writes:

On hearing I have been to Afghanistan, the educated Persian draws a deep breath, as though to restrain himself, expresses a polite interest in Afghan welfare, and enquires with feline suavity whether I found any railways, hospitals, or schools in the country. Hospitals and schools of course, I answer; all Islam has them; as for railways, surely steam is old-fashioned in a motoring age. When I told Mirza Yantz that the Afghans discussed their political problems frankly, instead of in whispers as here, he answered: "Naturally; they are less cultured than we Persians."

The Afghans return the dislike, but in different kind. Contempt, not jealousy, is all they feel.[1]

---

1   Byron, Robert, *The Road to Oxiana*. *Oxford University Press*, 2007, p. 126

There are throngs of people at the border in Islam-Qalah, mainly Afghans on their way home after decades in exile.

The UNHCR organizes repatriation of the Afghans who return to the country – last year alone they were almost 400,000 in number. Half of them had been deported, and half returned voluntarily. There were thousands of people every day during the summer, fewer in the winter. Those who return voluntarily receive assistance in the amount of 12 dollars per person for food, and 20 or 40 for transport to their home villages. Those who were forced to return receive nothing. They have to take up their bundles and manage as best they can.

I walk around among the big buildings that have been erected hastily by the UN, and talk to some of the refugees. The adults sit there with their belongings in a few bags, with tired eyes, surrounded by their many children. They have shoes on their feet and quilted jackets to shield them from the cold air. Quilted jackets – I had almost forgotten that they existed. A *patloo*, or blanket, against the cold is what tradition offers. A little girl in a woolen sweater sits eating a piece of bread that she's brought with her. In her lap she has a little Mickey Mouse purse, colorful and brand new. I haven't seen such well-dressed children since I came here. They shrug indifferently in response to my questions. The lanky, pimply interpreter I've hired for the day is having a hard time. Most of the children have lived their whole life in Iran and speak Persian rather than Dari, the Afghan dialect of the same language. Maybe he's just making things up; he looks so completely unengaged. I practically have to drag him around with me. As always, I feel vulnerable in this kind of situation. How I wish I could speak the language better, feel my own way and rely on my own judgment, instead of someone else's.

Many of the refugees have spent the two last decades in Iran; the children were born in refugee camps. They were forced to leave, my interpreter says. The war is over and now they have to go home. The Iranian officials no longer want to be responsible for health care or education, he explains.

As if those services awaited them here. Since Byron's days, hospitals and schools have declined. Do they really not know this? I wonder. A tough Afghan life is what awaits them. It's very possible that the family's house has burned down, or that someone else is living there. Maybe, just maybe the house has some electricity for a few hours now and then.

Panjshir [March/April 2005]

A gate of Soviet design closes off the dirt road to the mountain pass. A few bored soldiers from the Afghan Militia Forces are hanging about at the gate, which is decorated with a gigantic portrait of Ahmed Shah Massoud, the valley's own hero. Some tin helmets and machine guns are lined up on a table, ready for battle. The gate to Panjshir. I had imagined something more poetic.

A young man in a blue uniform and carrying a Kalashnikov shuffles up to the car. He scratches his neck, making his cap wiggle from side to side, and inspects our passports and permits from the Foreign Ministry.

Anne, a gangly, over-enthusiastic architect from Amsterdam who's leading the expedition, offers him some cigarettes, the universal parallel currency.

"Do you want tea? Black tea? Green tea?" asks the soldier when he finally hands back our passports.

"Thank you, no thank you," I answer.

"Next time."

His smile reveals three gold teeth, a small fortune in these parts, and he gives our driver the sign that we can go. Anne looks satisfied and slams the car door shut.

It's stunningly beautiful and the first day of spring. Sunny, with light clouds sprayed across the sky. We make our way through the mud along the narrow road, on our way toward a weekend of new scenery and mountain hikes. On one side is the massive mountainside of Hindu Kush, on the other, the swirling turquoise river. The war is woven into the landscape. Abandoned tanks sit wedged into the ground by the side of the road, or hang over the precipice down toward the river. Caterpillar vehicles tipped sideways separate one field from the next. An armored plate from the side of a car becomes a bridge over a creek. With a little earth on top, ammunition capsules serve as a veranda outside the village shop. I hope that they are empty.

Like a cross between Jesus, Bob Marley, and Che Guevara, Massoud looks down at me, with his pakol, or mushroom-shaped hat, and his cloudy gaze, from various places throughout the valley. The portraits of him, aside from the wrecked armored cars, are one of the few clues that I'm actually in the 21st century, or at least sometime after the invention of photography and ammunition. Other than that, the gate to Panjshir is like a time portal.

Le commandant Massoud, as the French call their golden boy, is a phenomenon. In spite of his reputation in the West as a moderate Mujahedin, he was a strong proponent of political Islam, like so many of his allies, and a central figure in the fundamentalist Islamic party *Jamiat-e Islami* and in the supervisory council Shura-e Nazar. To me, he was only one more in the depressingly long line of war criminals. He was the one of Professor Rabbani's commanders who held the highest rank, and when Rabbani became president in Kabul after the fall of the communist regime in April 1992, Massoud accepted the post of defense minister. The internal battles of different Mujahedin factions would soon lay waste to the capital. According to the human rights organization Human Rights Watch, some of the worst crimes against human rights during the war years happened between 1992 and 1993. The abuses documented in HRW's report from 2005 were orchestrated war crimes by troops under Massoud's control: "The attacks on civilians, summary executions, torture, abductions and looting ... were not spontaneous events or inevitable consequences of war. They were war crimes committed by troops within military structures with command-and-control mechanisms."[2]

But Massoud died just in time to retain his hero's halo. Two days before the World Trade Center attack, he was murdered in the Takhar province by two Al Quaeda-connected Arabs pretending to be journalists. And the rest of his confreres still remain intact

---

2 Human Rights Watch: *Blood-Stained Hands: Past Atrocities in Kabul and Afghanistan's Legacy of Impunity, 2005. www.hrw.org/ reports/2005/afghanistan0605/5.htm*

in their positions; if they are criticized at all it's in the softest of whispers.

After traveling for a few hours through the valley, we reach Dashtak, a handful of medium sized mud-brick houses squeezed in between the river and Hindu Kush. In one of these houses, we put down our bags in a room where we are to spend the night. The interior of the room slowly comes into focus, like a photograph in a developing bath, as my eyes adjust to the twilight. It is empty except for rugs on the floor and a pile of mattresses in a corner. A few flies buzz insistently. In the yard, a few cows, some chickens, and a turkey trudge aimlessly around. The whole village should be stamped "organically produced".

In the afternoon, we make a trip up the mountain near the village. I keep thinking about all the mines in Hindu Kush that the Russians were kind enough to drop from their planes during the war, and not even the stunningly beautiful snow-covered mountain tops reaching to the other side of the sky can calm me down. With every step, I grow more uneasy. Mobin, a young Pansjir resident with a bushy black beard and a lively gaze, tries to calm my fears.

"The people from the village go here every day."
I don't say anything.
"Every day they go here," he tries instead.
I'm silent.
He continues. He makes it sound as if all the villagers do nothing but run up and down the mountain all day. But I have my doubts. The villagers that I've seen stay close to their houses. The mountain is deserted. And calm can only come from within. Soon I no longer see any paths; we are trudging around in loose masses of gravel. The sight of an empty cartridge and the remainders of a grenade among the stones make me freeze up.

For a moment, the image comes back – my first meeting with a veteran from Afghanistan. It was in the metro in Moscow that I caught sight of him, so many years ago, during the last summer of the Soviet Union. He is sitting on a little board with wheels. He doesn't have any legs;

what's left of his trunk is dressed in uniform with polished buttons. Rows of pins on his breast jingle lightly when he moves. His army cap is lying upside down in front of him and three coins glitter in its red, silky lining. I don't dare meet his eyes, but the image of him has etched itself onto my retina forever. My own invisible tattoo that no one else can see, that I can never get rid of.

"Everything moves around this time of year, with the melting snow and the rain," I say to Mobin, with my eyes fixed on the slope.

He doesn't hear me, or pretends not to.

"Something that was OK yesterday might not be OK today," I repeat.

He nods. Confidently.

"But this mountain is fine," he says. "*Insh'allah* [God willing]."

I have no confidence whatsoever in Allah. If he exists, he's forgotten this land a long time ago. If he exists, he has no respect. I carefully place my booted foot inside Mobin's footstep and hold my breath. One step at a time, all the way back down into the valley and its safe clay road.

The next day, a new excursion in the mountains awaits us. I try to muster some courage, but I don't understand what I'm doing here on this weekend getaway among the landmines. There was a time when I could go to Pakistan instead, sit at a café and watch beautiful people passing by, stroll about in the shops. If there is one single thing I'm afraid of, it's mines. But I lace up my boots and go to the outhouse, trying to shoo away the rooster who wants to keep me company, in order to have at least two minutes completely to myself. I need to collect myself. A moment later we pile ourselves into the car and drive deeper into the valley. After half an hour, we have to stop at a police checkpoint.

"Permit!" says a local policeman, dressed in a woolen uniform with a familiar Soviet look about it.

Anne plays dumb. The policeman isn't swayed. *Pourquoi faire simple quand on peut faire compliqué?* Yes, why make it easy for yourself when you can make it complicated?

"There's a danger of landslides, and we have orders not to let anyone go into the valley," he says with an authoritative tone.

An unspoken *unfortunately* is left hanging in the air.

I look around for some trace of a communication channel through which the order might have reached this all-powerful police constable, some sign of cars or radios. But all I can see is an empty little shed, a tea kettle, and two of his colleagues. They are holding each other by the hand and shivering in the snow.

Anne tries a different tactic and becomes arrogant. That doesn't work either. An hour goes by. Here no one is pressed for time. Along with resignation, there's plenty of extra time. Ann confers with Mobin about appropriate bribes and appropriate ways to handle the transfer. But the policeman is irritated and offended and beyond the bribery stage. I sit in the backseat of the car and watch the men gesticulating out in the snow. All of a sudden, the gnawing feeling of anxiety in the pit of my stomach is gone. This will all work out. There won't be any minefield walk; I'll be able to keep my feet and legs.

Yet another half hour passes before even Anne gives up the idea of climbing the mountain. Instead we walk a few kilometers through the valley to Massoud's grave on a knoll not far from Jangalak. I don't take a single step outside the safety of the gravel path. We walk through one little village after another, all confusingly alike with their mud brick houses and herds of thick-tailed sheep. A shepherd makes his way with his sheep following after him, like a string of beads across the field. I stop and look at this interactive image of something that could just as well have been from the time of Jesus, or from 1383, the year that the Persian calendar shows now. On the village streets, flocks of children hang around, the boys in long shirts, the girls wearing little kerchiefs around their heads that make them look like Easter witches in Sweden. The boys push each other on homemade three-wheeled skateboards with wheels made of ball bearings scavenged from some armored car. Some of them play war with slingshots and stones. The carefully regulated *Consumer Reports*-world of my homeland feels awfully remote.

On the way, I'm accompanied by Mobin. He talks almost exclusively about Massoud. He wants to buy me a film about Massoud, and sit next to me and translate everything as I watch it, to make sure that I don't miss anything. To him, Massoud represents everything good, everything right and pure and principled – everything that is in such desperately short supply in Afghanistan.

The mausoleum is situated on a hill with a breathtaking view over the mountains and the valley below. There are quotes from the Koran, rugs, a flag draped over the grave. The green paint of the cupola has already begun to flake, and the flagstones under my feet rattle lightly.

"One day there will be many tourists here," says Mobin.

He nods toward the snow-covered mountain tops. The biggest force of all is self-deception, I think to myself, the dream of a different tomorrow. Such dreams are cheap and we carry them around with us all the time.

A call to prayer is heard across the valley – the soundtrack of their lives. The sincere, melancholy voice echoes between the mountainsides. We look around in the mausoleum and write in the guest book before sitting down to eat the lunch we've brought with us and then smoking on the hillside below. "Smoking kills slowly", reads the text on the cigarette packet. Yes, I know. Today I'm not in any hurry.

A Conference for All the Good People [March 2005]

As a "field representative", I've been invited to a conference in The Hague on the defense of human rights activists. It wasn't hard to persuade me. I'm flattered that someone in Stockholm has noted my existence and read my reports. And a trip to The Hague means that I can get out of the country for a few days, which is always good for me. It means that I can make a side trip to Stockholm. My tenant has given notice, and I've decided never to rent out my apartment again – ever. I want to have a base camp, a door to put my key in. An address to give new-found friends when our ways part.

The conference aims to discuss European Union Guidelines on Human Rights Defenders. For two days, we talk fervently about how important it is for the European Union to stand up for those who stand up for human rights. It's one long yawn – in a circle of likeminded people the discussion ends up being about as exciting as the annual Donald Duck Christmas special on Swedish TV. Everyone in the conference hall thinks that human rights are a good thing.

"Important!" we exclaim, filling our coffee cups.

And everyone agrees that the people who defend these rights are good, brave people.

"Fantastic!" we cry, nibbling a few more cookies, mainly because they're sitting there on the plates looking unwanted.

An Uzbek ruler or an Egyptian interrogation chief among the ranks of participants might have been able to stir up the debate, but as it is I struggle with sleepiness and a naked emperor, and a feeling of being the wrong person in the wrong profession in the wrong place.

"But what's the point?" I complain to a few other conference attendees during a break. "When it comes down to the line, when we have to pay a political price for our support of some local activist, we often chicken out anyway."

My colleagues exchange embarrassed glances over their coffee cups.

"A powerful punch in the air," I go on, waving the *Guidelines* in the air, a slim little book with thick, stiff paper, that someone has actually gone to the expense of printing and binding.

"It doesn't add anything that we're not already doing – when it suits us," I persist.

Before I know it, I'm left standing there by myself. I brush the cookie crumbs from my suit jacket and go in and sit down at my chair again. Scrutinizing.

This tendency to exaggerate and generalize – can't I ever learn to look at life a little more positively? Can't I realize that the game of negotiations that went into drawing up this watered-down booklet might actually move the world forward? Why can't I see it when everyone else here seems to be able to? It may happen slowly, but still – guidelines can be good to have, a good thing to refer to when some member nation wants to back out based on different interests. The chiding monologue in my head is soon completely overshadowed by my bad conscience. It gnaws at me. I should have manners enough to hide my lack of enthusiasm better. If nothing else, show a little gratitude for having been invited. Be as engaged as the other Swede here, my colleague Christoffer. He's walking around in his freshly pressed suit and well-ironed shirt, a little bit tight around the waist, and he is obviously Very Important. He strides back and forth carrying papers, preparing a presentation on the conclusions his working group has reached. I get an inferiority complex from less than that. But I'm not able to whip up any passion, only feelings of guilt. What am I doing here anyway? I should have stayed in Kabul and done something useful instead.

I buckle down through the next session and play hooky from the one after that. It's a chilly day with a scent of frost in the air, and I walk around aimlessly on the streets of The Hague, just breathing. For an hour or so I sit by the window of a café with a cup of coffee cooling in front of me, and stare out at the street, at the people who are hurrying past with their rosy cheeks and warm shoes. I try to make peace with myself. I remind myself that it is possible to make a difference. There are so many roles: actor, witness, observer, negotiator, representative, messenger, mediator, propagandist. It's just conference diplomacy that I seem to lack talent for. I promise myself to remember that, and to learn. Make a mental note. Something to avoid in the future.

The next day I take the plane to Stockholm. At Arlanda airport, I look over my shoulder before I throw away the book of guidelines in the nearest trash can. It's a wonderful feeling, and I can't suppress a smile.

I take the bus in to the city. The E4 highway sweeps by outside the window – I barely register the gray, cloudy, and dark March weather; I only have eyes for the straight edges of the lanes painted with reflective paint, the smooth asphalt, the instructive traffic markers, the illuminated signs pointing to all the shopping centers, the huge car dealerships. A feeling of warmth spreads throughout my body.

In the Well-Padded Home of the People [March/April 2005]

I'm at home in Stockholm again to split up the household. How I've longed to be home for a few days – if this really is my home. To cut across a lawn without thinking of landmines, to eat tangy Västerbotten cheese and rye bread – actually, to eat without feeling sick. To open my mouth and be able to express myself precisely, without missing any nuances, and without exertion, without having to think. The months in Kabul have made me like Stockholm more than ever. For every trip I make, I see Sweden in a new light.

On the metro, I'm intrigued by the teenage girls in miniskirts and tiny tops that leave half their stomach bare under the tight jackets. They talk and giggle, text and apply more lip gloss. Has the Stockholm transit agency introduced nudist cars? Or can people actually go out like this? Did they look like this back when I used to live here? My frames of reference have become so skewed, so twisted that it makes my head spin.

I have to split up the household by myself; Martin can't manage to participate. Or else he just doesn't want to. I spend a few hours in his apartment packing up my things at rocket speed, with one single thought in my head. *Don't make the practical emotional. Don't make the practical emotional.*

Then, when I'm done, and all the boxes and bags and things I haven't thought about in months are standing in the hallway of my old apartment on Karlbergsvägen, I lie down on the bed and take on the emotional part. I close my eyes, but the tears leak out anyway, instead of extinguishing the thing that's burning the inside of my eyelids. Me, alone, with holes in my soul so big that you could fly a plane through them.

By the next day, all of my self-pity seems to have flown away. I only want to enjoy every minute I'm here, do everything I've longed to do while I was over there on the other side of the globe. With the posture of a queen, I ride around the city and try to recreate the feeling of being home, feeling at home.

I meet Camilla at the trendy Café Creem on Karlbergsvägen. We've known each other since university, and we both ended up at the MFA. While I've been traveling around the world she's been working in Stockholm, with one year in Brussels. With a synthetic blanket on my lap and a half-liter latte in front of me, I sit and poke at a muffin the size of a handball.

"How is everything with you? What's it like in Afghanistan?"

"It's cold. You toughen up."

I could spend hours talking about Afghanistan, about the country that's teetering at the edge of the abyss, about the life I'm living, the people I meet. I could say that nowhere do you see life so clearly as when you're in the proximity of death. When the man with the sickle isn't breathing down your neck, he's at least passing by your neighborhood at regular intervals. But like so many times before, I stick to a few broad generalizations. What could you possibly find here to use as a starting point, in order to relate to what's happening over there?

"How are things with you? You look wonderful! How's the apartment sale going?" I ask instead.

To me, Camilla represents a refined type of normality. She lives with a decent, nice, clean-cut man. She's always stylish, always color-coordinated, and has a knack for home decor that makes me speechless.

"Fredrik and I went to look at houses on Lidingö over the weekend."

"And?"

"Nope. But I really hope we'll find something. I'm so tired of living in his apartment, and having all my things in storage."

Ah, a first-world problem I can sink my teeth into. And we talk about Camilla's and Fredrik's upcoming vacation and all their plans – so many plans that it makes me dizzy. Am I jealous of her relationship? Having a man to lean on, having someone to lean on? Not bearing everything by myself? I don't know. I don't know if I dare think about it. What if the answer is yes? What will I do with that knowledge, and those feelings? Maybe I should put in a personal ad. *Career woman looking for an ultra-social, well educated, fun guy without ambitions of his own, who wants to see the world. A plus if you enjoy logistics, cooking, and administration, and can get by for long periods of time without electricity. Wealth and good looks no obstacle.*

We talk for hours about design and shopping, and baby carriages that were delivered in the wrong color. And I don't want to talk about anything else. I want to wallow in shallow surfaces: fashion, design, and gossip from the MFA. I want to sit here in the warmth with my muffin and get to be someone else for a while. The other Diana.

A few hours later, we're standing in an antique shop, looking at a vase from the 1960s that costs 165 dollars.

"Oh, I've been looking for something like this."

I'm not convinced.

"But it's Stig Lindberg."

Never heard of the man.

"But does it look nice?"

165 dollars. How many monthly salaries is that for an Afghan? But I know the thought is silly, irrelevant.

Otherwise my clearest memory from this Stockholm visit is when a pipe in the bathroom of my newly reclaimed apartment sprang a leak.

I call up an emergency plumber. In through the door comes a bleached blonde girl in white painter pants clutching some tools in her fist. I can see her tattoo in the gap between her pants and her t-shirt, exactly where her lace thong splits into a T, as she struggles with the dripping pipe, sitting on her haunches in my little bathroom.

"There, all done," she says after a quarter of an hour.

I'm still standing in my entranceway, gaping, when she shuts the door behind her.

The days pass quickly, and soon it's already time to return to Afghanistan. I have an undisturbed 24 hours ahead of me. There's nowhere I have to go, no phone ringing, nothing to disturb my thoughts, and food will be served. I have my comfortable jeans, soft warm sweater, support stockings, a big scarf, my laptop, and a pile of books and magazines. Magazines where I can read articles about things like "How to fix your problem nails" and "How to be the best-looking woman in the bar". Earplugs, candy, and an iPod.

Curled up in my seat with *Vanity Fair* in my lap, I look down at Stockholm as it disappears beneath me. I've had my dose of Sweden; I feel sated. There's something so anxious about Stockholm, the conformity, the anxiety over not fitting in. It feels good to be leaving again, but a little melancholy at the same time. Am I one of those sad people who don't feel at home anywhere? Or am I one of those happy people who feel at home everywhere? Today I'm leaning toward the latter. And I can't escape the feeling that it's easier to be a stranger in Kabul than in Stockholm, where I should feel at home.

"So you're going to London?" asks the salesman type next to me when the stewardesses have passed out our trays with little dishes of mysterious food.

"No, to Kabul."

I bite my lip as I realize my mistake. All I want is to be left alone, but now I've set the stage for a discussion of oppressed women and the Americans' war on terror, which could last all the way to our landing at Heathrow.

"But what are you doing in Kabul?"

I look at him, weighing my alternatives. I've read somewhere that the best way to escape chatty fellow passengers is to tell them you're a fundraiser for the Scientologists. Would he believe that the Scientologists are active in a Muslim country where converting from Islam means a death penalty? No, it's too late, and I'm terrible at lying.

"I work there, I'm a diplomat," I say with a sigh.

He gives a little start, as if I had stuck him with a needle.

"You?"

All his doubt has stuck to those three letters, and now it's too late to do anything about it. We both heard it.

"Yes, me."

"Oh. Well, I mean – why not?"

He gives a little laugh, wrinkles his forehead and pauses, realizing he's dug himself even deeper.

He looks at me, more intently now.

"Why not what?"

The image of the luxurious life that diplomats are expected to live around the world doesn't mesh with my worn out nail polish and my seat way back in tourist class. The Scientology story would have been easier to sell.

"No, I mean, not at all, I just thought that..."

He falls silent again. I never get to know what he thought; I'll just have to guess. That deeply rooted idea that everything is so much more elegant than it really is, a carefully cultivated myth. Aristocratic, spoiled elites – preferably men – with double-breasted suits, distinguished looks, and graying temples. Men who address each other as "brother" and gorge themselves on caviar and champagne. And here I am, with my messy hair and a half-empty glass of juice made from concentrate in front of me – not aristocratic, no more spoiled than he is by having happened to be born in Sweden.

For a moment, just a little too long, the hum of the airplane spreads out between us, as we each concentrate on splitting open our pale rolls with blunt plastic knives.

"And you? Do you often travel to London?" I ask. "It's such a lovely city!"

Then I add my nicest smile, as a garnish.

I should have called him out for his narrow-mindedness. But no, I don't bother. It's been said that diplomacy is not about being right, it's about pleasing. I disagree, but let it go this time. I can deal with a little small talk as we eat; then I want to be left alone, and read about what to do with my split nails.

A WOMAN'S LOT [APRIL 2005]

"**W**hat did you choose?" I ask the women, as tea, fried eggs, and bread are served up on the rug in front of me.

"A diesel generator," they say.

For one odd moment. I lose my power of speech. Then:

"A diesel generator? Is a diesel generator really the thing you want most of all?"

They nod. It's quiet for a moment.

"What do the men want, then?"

I dip some bread in the egg yolk, take a sip of tea. Wait.

"The diesel generator."

They don't even squirm, just look at me with their friendly, curious eyes.

Some colleagues and I are on a visit to a women's shura in Durani, in the Wardak Province. The shura was formed in an attempt to create new structures for decision-making, and to give citizens some influence over part of the billions in aid money given to Afghanistan. Among the village families, representatives are chosen for two shuras – one for men and one for women. Each village receives a sum of money and the shuras decide what to do with it. The women's shuras receive ten percent of the village money, the men ninety. And yet, they want a diesel generator.

"A diesel generator?" I ask again.

Yes, indeed. At first, they had thought about sewing machines and a girls' school, but then they realized that they also wanted a diesel generator – since that's what the men wanted.

"Absolutely. A diesel generator."

Everyone nods in agreement.

"Who's going to pay for the diesel?" someone asks.

"And the maintenance?" someone else asks.

All of these life questions without answers.

No, there is no girls' school in the village, and neither girls nor women are allowed to go outside the village. The harsh atmosphere of tradition contains no oxygen for such radical ideas. In-justice is embedded like an anchor in the bedrock of tradition. Every woman must be accompanied by a *maharam*, a male family member, if she has to leave her home for some reason – even if this *maharam* is just a five-year-old boy. The men's total control over the female body, over femininity and female sexuality, is a cornerstone of the Afghan culture. Like most other women in the country, therefore, these women live under what can only be called lifelong house arrest. Because of this, they were also unable to vote, they explain, when I ask if they participated in the presidential election.

We leave the subject of politics and move on to those things that are the lot of every Afghan woman: children, family, the home. No, there is no midwife. And they aren't allowed to go to the medical center in the village a few kilometers away – not that they could afford it anyway.

"At least two of us will die in childbirth this year," says a woman of about thirty.

I don't detect anything in her face when she says this, matter-of-factly, drily. It's just one of life's many realities.

In Afghanistan, over 99 percent of the women marry, many of them against their will. In the countryside, the age of marriage is between twelve and sixteen; in certain provinces, as low as ten. In most countries, many of the teenage marriages in Af-ghanistan would be considered pedophilia, but here they go unremarked.

The marriages are usually arranged matches, in which the girls are used as a way to secure loyalties and clan relationships. After the fall of the Taliban regime, the custom of rival clans exchanging women and girls as compensation in settlements, or to regulate debts of various kinds, has been adopted again. For example, a murder can be atoned for by having the murderer's family give a daughter to the victim's family. This isn't a gesture of conciliation, but rather is intended to dishonor the murderer's family, and consequently these girls and women are kept under slave-like conditions in their new household.

It turns out that two of the women in the circle on the floor where I'm sitting are married to the same man. The older one is toothless and wrinkled as if she were a hundred years old; the other one must be ten years younger than I am. I don't dare think about how old the man is.

"It's no fun when your husband takes another wife, whom he likes better," a worn-faced girl of about twenty explains.

The old woman chews some bread and stares straight ahead with dead eyes. She doesn't say anything.

The time is starting to run out. We get up from the rug and thank the women before moving on to have lunch with the governor of the province. On the way, we drive by a village that melts in to the mountainous landscape, with its houses behind high mud walls. This is what they look like, the villages where twelve-year-old girls are sold to men, sometimes fifty years older than they are. This is what they look like, the unremarkable houses where private civil wars continue to rage, where some girls try to set fire to themselves to escape their miserable lives. If the girl survives her burn wounds, she has nowhere to go. The family will reject her. And for a woman without family, an abyss opens up. All that remains for her is begging, prostitution, or life in a *maraston*, a kind of poorhouse where the poorest of the poor are mixed with the mentally ill, the physically handicapped, and drug addicts. Buried alive in the culture's mass grave.

A few minutes later we reach Maidan Shahr, the capital of Wardak Province. But the word 'capital' gives the wrong impression. Maidan Shahr consists of a few mud houses, some gasoline pumps, and two or three shabby concrete buildings that house the provincial administration. It's a collection of buildings that embody desperation and idle poverty. On all sides, achingly beautiful mountains surround the godforsaken hole.

The governor's building lacks both electricity and water, but the newly appointed governor, Abdul Jabar Naeemi, is as exuberant as a child. Impeccably dressed in a suit, he receives us in his simple office, which is dominated by hundreds of plastic flowers in the gaudiest shades of the color spectrum.

"Welcome! It's so wonderful to have you here! There's so much to talk about!" he says, as he settles down in a puffy armchair and crosses his legs.

The creases in his trousers are so sharp that you could highjack planes with them.

"These are a gift from the people," he says apologetically, waving toward the truly awful flower decorations that he sees we have noticed. "I don't want to remove them, someone might be offended."

We talk about the situation in the province. There's essentially nothing there, but Governor Naeemi won't let himself be discouraged by that. He has plenty of ideas about what should be done, and just as many ideas about how to carry out his plans. Above all, he wants to build schools and make sure that some of the province's hundreds of teachers receive at least some training.

"Otherwise the children won't learn anything."

I can't help but agree.

We dig in to lunch – fried rice, raw vegetables, and piles of chicken drumsticks. But soon Naeemi himself has to get up from his half-eaten meal; some new delegation is waiting impatiently outside the door.

"I'm sorry, I'm sorry. Excuse me. I just need to hear what they have to say ..."

He disappears out the door.

"There's hope," I say to Nadjla, our interpreter.

His enthusiasm and eagerness to work give me a bubbling feeling of happiness.

"A suit and tie won't save this country," she mutters.

After lunch, we roll a hundred meters from the governor's building to the police headquarters, where we're met by the acting police chief, a man without insights, goals, or opinions. His hand slips toward mine when we greet each other. He's wearing a too-tight Soviet wool uniform with a lot of stars on the epaulettes.

The office decor could be straight from a Soviet Union version of a 1973 Ikea catalog, if there had been such a thing. I'm sure the shabby, crooked table could be exchanged for a couple of hundred dollars at some chic retro design shop, if you could only manage to get it home.

"Things are good here," he says, as he looks me straight in the eye.

"There are no problems here," he continues, poking at some papers on his desk.

"Everyone is cooperating. We have everything we need."

The only problem that sticks out amid the snowy slush is the low salaries. Many of the policemen have to go home for the day as early as one o'clock. Sometimes they don't come at all.

"You have to make allowances for them," says the acting police chief, as he glances at the clock.

It's already past four.

We hurry onward. The driver brakes in front of what looks like a ruin, but turns out to be the public prosecutor's office. The provincial prosecutor, Abdul Ahmad, is sitting in his office in the only part of the building where the roof has not caved in. He invites us to sit down on the couch. Like the governor, Abdul Ahmad is newly appointed, but more resigned than enthusiastic about the challenges his new job presents. Powerlessness is embedded in every word. The prosecutor's office can't do its job at all, he says. They lack any means of carrying out investigations. They don't have transportation to the crime site, technical equipment, or legal texts. Only two percent of his staff is educated.

"You have to be happy if the rest have even finished twelfth grade," he says with a defeated smile.

As the agency's most experienced worker, he receives 2,300 afghanis, or 37 dollars, per month.

For a minute or two we ponder this fact in silence.

"It isn't even enough for transportation out to the districts to carry out an investigation when something happens," he says at last.

"So you have no budget for your work?" I ask.

No, no. None at all.

I wonder what they do all day. What exactly happens with the common crimes of the province – which, according to the provincial prosecutor himself, include assault, murder, human trafficking, kidnappings? But I don't even bother asking, because I already know the answer: Nothing.

A Rare Visit [April 2005]

My father and two of my younger sisters, Helga and Gerda, are going to come and visit me. I'm so happy that they're coming. God knows there aren't exactly a lot of visitors here. I desperately want someone at home to have seen a little glimpse of my existence, my everyday life. I want them to see how I am, how I'm living, see my nice little house. I want Dad to not worry (if he does), and to understand that I'm doing fine here.

Helga is sick when she arrives. She looks like an unhappy little doll, her big eyes shiny with fever. She's mostly quiet, but Gerda and Dad talk. Through them, I see the city through the eyes of a stranger again.

"It looks terrible. How poor it is! What's that?"

Gerda points through the car window to a big tent a little off the road. Once it was white, but now it's a dingy gray color and the fabric hangs down in tatters.

"A school," I answer. "It's a school."

"Ugh, cold in the winter and boiling hot in the summer," Dad snorts.

Always so practical.

"Well, yes," I say. "But it's better than no school at all..."

One of the most important changes since the Taliban's fall from government is the fact that millions of children can now go to school.

"Does anyone live in those houses?" Gerda asks as we roll by what looks to me at this point like an ordinary house. A bit small and dilapidated, maybe, with a very crooked door – but still, a house.

"Well, yes..."

It's not that bad, I'm thinking, as I try to come to terms with my role as Defender of Kabul. Can't they focus a little more on all the positive things? No big yellow discount superstore like in Ullared, no theme restaurants, no Robinson reality show...

The car brakes at my house and we get out. Najib, my *chaukidar*, or watchman, greets us, and I introduce everyone. He's enthusiastic and just as pleasant as always. Before anyone has time to react, he's already carried all the luggage into the house.

Dad walks around the house, inspecting all the gates and the bars on the windows.

"Listen, is it really safe to live here all alone?"

"Oh, yes. It's OK."

"But shouldn't you have some kind of guard?"

I see that he's looking at Najib, who's sitting on a chair in his gym shoes, staring straight ahead of him at nothing in particular. It's taken a good deal of time to argue that we should have real locks and a serious security company for our houses, with armed guards at night. Not just a tired man who sleeps on a mattress in the back of the house to no avail, the way it used to be at the office building.

"I have guards in the evening and night," I explain. "Najib is mostly here when I'm at work, so the house isn't empty and unwatched."

My father makes a grunting sound. I can't escape the feeling that I'm suddenly defending myself all the time. *Don't you dare come here and be condescending and question Afghanistan, my beloved Afghanistan!*

There isn't much to do in Kabul – the tourist trade has lost its grip. We see those shards of the city that are still left to be seen. We go to the few nice restaurants there are. Then we go there again, since there aren't very many. We stop by my office and greet my colleagues. We go shopping on Chicken Street. We watch pirated DVDs from Pakistan. We have long and serious discussions about where the country, the region, and the world are headed. We read, spend time together, and drink coffee. We console ourselves with wine and toast Afghanistan's future.

One evening we're sitting in my living room drinking our evening tea. The gas burner, turned up as high as possible, gives out a faint hiss; it's pleasant and warm. Gerda, Helga, and I have just finished watching a movie, Dad is already asleep. We talk about the movie, and then we talk about this and that, until one of those gaps in the natural flow of conversation comes up. It isn't a painful silence – these are my sisters – but we all hold our breath for a moment, waiting.

"So what have you been doing all these months? What do you do when you're off work, anyway?" Gerda says slowly, finally.

They're both watching me now, as if I were a stranger. Friendly and curious gazes, a little more alert than they were than a moment ago.

"I work out, go out with my friends, watch DVDs..."

It's not the whole truth, but for some reason I want it to sound like any other city, any other life. I prefer not to have free time. My work absorbs me, and I let myself be absorbed. I know that my work will take me hostage if I don't watch out. Work and free time blend into each other; my colleagues become my friends. My work defines not only how I earn my living, but also where I live, in what country, in what city, so far away from everything that used to be my environment. I'm thankful that I've had the opportunity to come here, and that I have a job that takes me to places like this. I don't want to live with my back turned to the world; I want to try to understand things. I want to form my own opinion through personal meetings, by seeing things for myself. I want to put facts in their context, look at the actors and their interests and think about what it means for Sweden or for Europe. I want to provide information that is independent of other countries and other economic or political interests to those decision makers who want to read it.

It's important for me to try to understand Afghanistan, in order to understand how we, as in "the international community", best should act, and how Sweden could move in that direction. Pretentious, maybe, but that's how it is.

"Oh, I don't know. The weeks go by so fast here," I answer briefly. I stretch and yawn, then get up and start putting things away. "I'm going to bed. Sleep well, and see you tomorrow."
Insh'allah.

As the days go by, insight dawns. I had imagined that it would be easier for them to understand if they only came here. If they saw that life went on as usual here, or in any case saw that here, too, there's an everyday life, just like anywhere else. They would see that I'm doing fine, with a job, friends, some free time. But when I see Dad's, Gerda's, and Helga's skepticism and their pitying looks, I realize that I was completely wrong. They only see the things that I barely notice anymore. For example, that my bakery sits on a garbage dump. That everything, everywhere, is broken. That the electric current, if there's any at all, is so weak that it can't light up a room. That my little grocery store on the corner a few blocks away is out of most things, that the dates on the packages have expired. They see the need that cries out from the thin bodies and the shabby houses. They see the armored vehicles, the cement barriers, the roadblocks, all the forewarnings of so many dangers, of all the things that might happen. At this point they all feel sorry for me and are worried about me.

"I wish you had time to see something else besides Kabul," I sigh. "It's so gray here this time of year. Afghanistan is more than this, it's not just sackcloth and ashes..."

They look at me doubtfully, silently.

That's how I come up with the idea of traveling along the land route to Islamabad, where they'll catch their flight back to Europe.

"Then you'll get to see the incredibly beautiful landscape, mountains that will take your breath away!"

Silence.

"And then we'll drive across the legendary Khyber Pass! I've always wanted to see it!" I say, in an attempt to inspire my dubious listeners.

Ever since I traveled around in Kyrgyzstan and Uzbekistan one boiling hot summer with Peter Hopkirk's *The Great Game* in my hand, the Khyber Pass has had a special ring in my ears, an echo of British spies, adventures, and camel caravans packed with ammunition, cigars, and champagne. Rudyard Kipling called it a sword-cut through the mountains. Trade caravans and armies have come and gone here through the centuries.

"The what pass?" asks Helga.

Young people! Whatever. It'll be something to remember – oh, yes.

The day before, I make sure to call around and ask about the security situation along our travel route. Yes, it should be OK to drive a car the way we had planned, is the picture I get, as long as you drive during the day.

"I think it's a bad idea," Dad says in his most severe voice, the one he uses for talking to stubborn children.

Gerda and Helga don't say much of anything.

"It's OK," I say. "I've talked to all kinds of people, it's OK."

Dad sulks. Helga and Gerda don't exactly let out cries of joy either. But I persist.

"It's OK," I repeat. "It'll be fun!"

I don't know what it is about me and vacations. For me, they've never been about resting and having a good time, as much as seeing something different. Places that make you heave a sigh of relief when you're back in your normal life. Places that remain sharp in your memory years later. Places that give you perspective on your regular life. When my colleagues drove around Lake Como, or went clubbing in Barcelona, I've taken the bus through the Albanian countryside, or trudged along Ashgabat's desolate streets looking for something to eat.

"It'll be interesting," I correct myself.

"Maybe you and I can go, but I don't want Helga and Gerda to go. They'll have to take the plane," Dad says in his most authoritative voice.

So two family members can be sacrificed on the altar of adventure, but not four? Would Helga and Gerda attract too much Taliban attention? No. I don't feel like asking about the logic in this.

"It's fine, Dad, it's OK! It'll be fun for you to see some of the country too. Not just gray Kabul," I continue stubbornly, desperate to sell Afghanistan as quite a fantastic place, in spite of everything.

Just you wait...

Dad looks at me, suppresses a grimace. He's not convinced.

After a lot of nagging, I get what I want. Of course. This is my 'hood, these are my contacts, I'm the one who knows something.

Dad is annoyed, but he knows that he's lost the battle. He's completely in my hands. I book a car and driver to take us to the Afghan-Pakistani border.

We get started early in the morning, in order to make it to Islamabad, or at least Peshawar, before dark. Najib drags our luggage outside and waves goodbye. Will he sit there behind the wall for days, staring emptily in front of him? Sometimes I actually envy him his lack of ambition. Sometimes I feel like a barge driver. What's the point of my own striving anyway? All my eagerness to see, learn, travel, understand, the restlessness I can never escape from? All the early mornings and late nights? It seems like the end result has mostly been parasites, harder to get rid of every time, and vitamin deficiencies. Eating cauliflower for months, before the apricots and pomegranates finally come. Endless watermelon. Conserves and tea. Nuts and expired couscous. But I can't do anything else. I don't want anything else but to have it like this. It's at once so simple and yet so hard to accept.

We soon leave Kabul, and then the road is replaced by a bumpy washboard. Mile after mile, hour after hour we shake along. On the better stretches we make 45 kilometers an hour. I can't remember when time passed this slowly.

When we finally reach the Khyber Pass, I barely notice it. I'm shaken up enough as it is. *Look, there's the old British fort – yes, yes, some stones among all the other stones, yes. Or is that something else, maybe? Have we already passed the fort? Or what?* The car shakes on further, like a skittish horse.

At the border in Torkham it's utter chaos. Cars, flower-painted trucks with surrealistically big loads. People everywhere. They pull at our car doors until the car rocks, and press their noses against the glass when they can't open them. Dad seems to appreciate the spectacle, while Helga just shrinks into her seat, and Gerda asks again and again how I can stand to live here. I gather up our passports and slide out of the car. How I can stand to live here? It just is what it is, nothing to make a fuss over.

Our driver from Kabul helps us find a new taxi that can take us on to Islamabad – if we even make it there before dark. He settles on a big, truculent man who has a minibus with broken seats. We agree on a price.

"This will be fine, yes?" I say.

It's not a question.

"Then we'll have a little more legroom than on the way here."

End of discussion.

I negotiate with the border police or whoever they are, the men in assorted uniforms. (Who's to say that uniforms have to be uniform?) They offer us tea and nuts and little cookies. They want to marry off Gerda. I urge them to get on with things, smile, keep repeating that they should stamp the passports and do whatever they have to do, so that we can move on.

"You must have a soldier with you in the car."

"Yes, OK, whatever."

"And it will cost something."

What a surprise.

Time passes – all these people who tug at me, offer me more nuts, get involved, have an opinion. And yet nothing seems to happen.

"Well, that was no match," I say briskly as we finally leave the twilight zone behind us.

Don't ask me how it happened.

The man who's driving the dirty minibus is silent. In the front seat sits a soldier with a rifle between his knees and a beret the size of a well cover on his head. He stares stiffly ahead; maybe he has a stiff neck. I don't know exactly where he's from – I assume it's from the paramilitary group the Khyber Rifles, who are trying to maintain whatever control can be achieved in Khyber Agency. If he needs a ride home, I don't want to get in his way. Besides, it's thanks to him that we're allowed through the many checkpoints where we get stopped along the way.

The minutes drag on, dark falls. I can feel that my store of trust with the family has sunk to a new low. *What are we doing here? What's wrong with flying?* I smile bravely.

"We'll have to spend the night in Peshawar."

When we roll into Peshawar it's pitch black, like a grave. The driver can't find his way in the city and is completely unwilling to help us find the address of a hotel that I've jotted down. On further thought, it wouldn't be a good idea for him to drive around in the dark, asking for directions, with us foreigners in the car. Instead, we stop at a shabby hotel along the main road leading from the border. The sign beckons with the name Grand Hotel. One small part grand hotel, the rest a pit. Yes, there's certainly room. I haggle over the price for a while until we agree. Drawing a sigh of relief, I turn to pay the driver and send him away.

He stuffs the bills in his pocket and reaches out his hand again.

"No, no," I say.

His gaze has fixed on the rest of the bills in my hand.

"No! You got everything, even though you did not take us all the way to Islamabad."

We haggle with body language. The mood is oppressive. A feeling of despondency steals over me.

When I come down to the foyer a little later, he's still there. He wants more money.

"Can you help me translate?" I ask the thin man at the reception desk.

He nods.

"Explain that he has received what we agreed, even though he has taken us to Peshawar only. Not Islamabad!"

Why does my English regress when I'm talking to people who probably can't understand me? As if it were any easier for them to understand English with the wrong word order, the wrong endings, and the wrong tenses.

The two men look silently at each other. And then at me.

"Please, explain. No more money. Finish. Tomorrow we take other taxi."

A flood of words fills the shabby reception area. Our driver is angry, you don't need to know Urdu to understand that. Or is it Pashto? It doesn't make much difference, he's angry in any case. A clock is ticking on the wall and the sound fills the gaps that arise in the heated tangle of words.

"No more money," I say, shaking my head.

"Already paid too much. Too, too much."

Lively discussion ensues. If a bad mood could be measured with an instrument, the instrument would be broken by now, as if an elephant had stepped on a scale made for human beings. I don't understand anything else from the exchange besides what I already know – he wants more money. But no, he's not getting it. He's received what we agreed on.

I dig around in my purse for my cell phone so I can call the embassy in Islamabad and tell them that we're not coming tonight. And tell them the name of the area where we were dropped off. Not that it helps, but just for the sake of doing it. Because it seems like the smart thing to do. But my cell phone is gone.

A quick trip out to the empty minibus, and I return triumphantly with the cell phone, which had fallen down between the seats.

"If he'd just driven away, he would have gotten a cell phone too," Gerda says with a harsh laugh.

See, just a couple of days here in the mountains and already she's thick-skinned, hardened.

Our driver looks angrily at me. Then finally he drives away. It doesn't make the unpleasantness disappear, but at least it moves out of sight.

The next day we drive on to Islamabad, where we spend a magical day. We go on an excursion to Taxila, where we climb around among the ruins from 600 BCE, accompanied only by a shepherd and his flock. We shop for shawls in the softest pashmina and dozens of DVDs in Jinnah Supermarket.

In the evening, we eat a good dinner at the home of a colleague. The feeling is relaxed, happy, as if my dear family had escaped the grip of the devil.

"My God, how nice it is to be back in Pakistan," they all three chirp.

Well, it isn't all that special, is it? I think to myself, feeling stung.

The next day, my family flies home to Sweden and I fly back to Kabul. I sit there downhearted in the UN plane, feeling like an unsuccessful vacuum cleaner salesman. I promise myself not to insist on more visits.

Interior Decorating [May 2005]

"Zaki-jan, could you please help me hang these two pictures on the wall? Right here?"

I mark the spot on the wall where I want them with two post-it notes.

Zaki is the office handyman, and he has just been at my home to inspect my electrical cabinet, which had caught fire earlier.

"Yes, Miss Diana."

"I want them to hang next to each other, at the same height."

"Yes, Miss Diana."

"Thank you, that's super."

When I come home to eat lunch, the pictures are hanging on the wall, more or less where I wanted them to be, but the right picture is at least five centimeters lower than the left one.

"Zaki, could you be so kind and come over to my house?"

I put down the cell phone with a sigh, and take a few deep breaths.

Zaki is there in two minutes.

"I asked you to hang them at the same height."

Zaki looks at me without comprehending.

"Yes, Miss Diana?"

"But now the one on the right is lower than the one on the left," I point out.

Zaki looks at the wall, then at me. Still not comprehending.

"Would you mind re-doing it? I want to have them at the same level – not five centimeters difference, not one, not a half. The same. Exactly the same."

"Yes, Miss Diana."

"Is anything unclear?"

"No, Miss Diana."

Zaki smiles; he's always just as helpful.

Two days later, we're still at it. It must be the fifth try. Or the seventh. Each time we get a little closer, each time Zaki is a little unhappier, each time it's harder for me to hide my irritation. It isn't the words that betray me, it's my sharp voice. I'm not nice at all anymore. I only feel like beating up the man. How hard can it be? All the worst sides of me – and one thing I've discovered here in this country is that they are unpleasantly and surprisingly many – come out in full bloom after too many weeks in one place. I breathe deeply. I count to ten. Nothing helps. I need to get away from here, out. Away.

Finally, the pictures are hanging on the wall. There's only two or three millimeters' difference when I give up. The wall behind the pictures looks like a sponge, full of little holes. I try to tell myself that there are different ways of doing things. I tell myself that precision isn't the main thing here – it's the broad brushstrokes that count. Like survival. I tell myself that I have a tendency to get stuck on small and irrelevant details – a few centimeters or millimeters or decimeters here or there – because I've never had anything more important to do. And if I weren't trying to escape from the hysteria of home decorating, why am I even standing here on an Oriental rug in my entranceway, arguing about some pictures? But still: Here we have a little know-how in its most basic form, and yet I've failed. I can't help wondering how the transfer of knowledge and concepts is working in other areas. It looks so simple in the policy papers – to build up Afghan capacity. *As long as they do things the way we do them, it will all work out, everything will be fine.* But how do you do that? When we, that is, the international community, are going to help the Afghans build up a national army, and an independent judicial system? Sometimes I privately wonder if our presence here doesn't have the opposite effect. We take the country's few literate, educated people with knowledge of other languages and make them guides, drivers, and general fixers. Surgeons, teachers, lawyers. Will Zaki, the next time someone asks him to hang something in a specific place, measure carefully, and then check again, before he puts the drill to the wall? Will he do a careful and good job? Maybe. Probably not. On the other hand, the odds are pretty high that I will fix whatever needs to be fixed by myself next time, to spare my nerves. Because Zaki might be busy doing and re-doing something else he's been told to fix, without really understanding how or why.

Afterwards I can't quite shake off my feeling of frustration. I feel irritated, pessimistic, helpless. Like a child who can't make myself understood, I just want to scream. I know there's only one thing to do – try to get away for a few days. For my own sake, and for the sake of those around me.

Fashion. Glamour. Lifestyle.
[May 2005]

Airports tend to look so oddly alike. Anxious, rushed travelers looking into the distance and with too many things to keep track of – shopping bags, purses, slips of paper. The same old assortment in the tax-free shops, like a dismal foreshadowing of where globalization can lead us. Lavazza coffee in Havana. Prada perfume in Kigali. Montblanc pens for a year's wages in Dushanbe. But the airport in Islamabad has none of this urban, worldly, slick surface. The few kiosks that there are sell wall clocks with quotes from the Koran, piles of knickknacks, and locally produced candies. A man with a dragging gait pulls a duty-free cart stocked with cigarette packs and Pakistan's version of Barbie dolls, without miniskirts or swimsuits, back and forth through the departure hall. Clusters of bored Pakistani men sit around fanning themselves with their boarding passes in the oppressive air, dressed in shalwar kamiz in creamy white or light gray, in a space that reminds me of an overcrowded, sleepy dormitory. I see only one woman. Her face is hidden behind a scarf, carefully fastened with safety pins. Except for the pistachio-shaped eyes and well-plucked brows, her hands are the only exposed skin. They are decorated with henna painting and gold rings. *Some things will never be different*, sings Kele Okereke in my iPod. He's absolutely right.

I order tea from one of the waiters who are bustling around in white uniforms and bowties.

"A hundred rupees," says the server.

He holds out his hand, carefully avoiding my gaze.

"But last time it was twenty-five," I exclaim with surprise.

"OK then, twenty-five."

He snatches the bills with a sigh. It's a sigh that encapsulates a feeling of world-weariness and resignation.

I sip my tea, which is as turgid as raw oil and so strong that it could be an acceptable alternative to Ecstasy. The feeling of being on a journey spreads through my body. I inhale the air, saturated with expectation. Over there, will it be different? Better? These sugarcoated daydreams and hopes – so bittersweet. I could sit here for hours.

Unsurprisingly, when we finally take off from Islamabad's airport, the flight is very delayed.

"We have big technical problems," the pilot announces over the raspy loudspeaker system by way of an excuse, as he taxis the plane away for takeoff.

I fidget with the thin piece of paper that serves as my boarding pass, and look around the crowded cabin. The Pakistani man in the seat next to me looks as doubtful as I'm feeling. He fingers his prayer beads, mumbling. But God in his heaven, at a pleasant distance from life's problems and unexpected turns, doesn't concern himself with Pakistani technology.

With a battered soul, I'm on my way to Dubai for a few days of bliss. I don't know what to expect. I have no expectations, I only know that I need to breathe something besides Afghanistan air for a few days.

The hotel is better than anything my imagination could have conjured up in the dust of Kabul. There's a bellman at the door, in a uniform so heavily starched that it could stand up by itself. Men in garments that look like nightgowns, headdresses, and Rolex watches glide about the marble-covered hotel lobby to the music from the grand piano. They talk in Arabic as their ultra-modern cell phones beep. The air is filled with heavy perfume and the apathy of comfort. Five stars feel like fifteen. I can't take my eyes off the polished floor, where all the marble stones are laid with such precision that not only is it absolutely level, but all the stones seem to be perfectly spaced from each other as well. It's smooth and slick, and as shiny as a curling course.

Dubai is all about *Fashion. Glamour. Lifestyle.* – at least if you can believe the ad in the glass elevator that whisks me up to my room. Fine with me. I'm already sold, I already want to move here. I'll emigrate – maybe I'll become a journalist based in Dubai, and write well-informed, probing articles about the weapons trade and illegal migration. Or maybe a consultant. Or a personal shopper for rich Russians who come here.

My room is the size of a dancehall. The view is brilliant. The TV has more channels than I can count. I zap through a few of them until I'm confronted with the outside world. The camera quickly pans over a boy who has lost his legs in an explosion in Baghdad. What's left of the leg stumps looks like they're filled with sausage stuffing. Freedom is untidy, as Rumsfeld so aptly put it. This is what it looks like, democracy on the march. And the hunt for cheap oil, of course. But just for today, I don't have the energy to look at it.

I turn off the TV and return to the marble lobby. I love hotels. I could spend my whole vacation right here – sit in the lobby, ensconced in the comfortable couch with magazines, books, and my laptop, and chat with other visitors.

I drink coffee and pick at a piece of chocolate cake as I clear my senses of both grit and compassion. I thumb through a magazine with thick glossy paper and seductive pictures. I sit there for a while to acclimate myself before venturing out into the crowds. I look at all the smiling people who nod at me. Friendly Asian women pour me more coffee with a pleasantly discreet manner and invite me to order more from the menu. I smile back, comfortably reclined against the pillows. Kabul suddenly feels far away. It feels like I've never been there – irrelevant, unimportant.

After coffee, I take a stroll up to the rooftop pool. I feel blindingly white, like the fluorescent lights in a solarium, as I slip into a deck chair under a parasol. The woman next to me at the edge of the pool is baked brown and has perfectly waved hair. Her bikini is so tiny that I have to look twice to find it. She's reading an article with the title "How to Marry a Millionaire" through her enormous sunglasses. Something tells me that she's come to the right place. For just a moment I wish that I had at least an ounce of her sense of purpose, a tiny bit of her ability to focus on the essential things in life. Dubai is the Mecca of exaggeration, of consumption as religion and as meaning in life. This is where wealthy Russians come with bulging attaché cases and buy apartments for 45 million dollars cash. This is where there are special training pools for camels to strengthen their leg muscles.

On the other side of me lies a woman in a lipstick-red swimsuit and a teased hairdo. She is clearly the type of person who never sweats or gets wrinkles in her pants or ketchup on her blouse. Small talk pearls out of her expertly painted mouth, as she chirps into her cell phone.

"Oh really!" she laughs.

The tightly stretched smile threatens to split her face into two less attractive parts.

"That is fantastic!" she continues, revealing her bleached teeth.

The woman must have so much joy, success, money, and fancy schools in her resume that I'm afraid she can never be interesting. But she seems pleasant – charming, even.

And what fingernails. I must call the reception desk right away and ask where I can get a manicure. And pedicure, and maybe some massage too.

The next day I take a taxi to the shopping boulevard at the Emirates Towers. On the car radio, commercial pop music dances its victory dance across the world, at the wheel sits yet another Pakistani guest worker. Through the car window, I see wealth everywhere. The sun adds luster to the city, like in an expensive travel brochure printed on thick glossy paper. Architecture that breathes soulless perfection. Asphalt that glitters in the sharp light. Well-swept streets, electricity, smooth concrete. Women dressed in light tops and short skirts. The place is a balm for my wounded soul, long ago drained of any content it may once have held.

I stroll around in the shops. A child of my time, I'm soon sucked into the commerce. I stroke Louis Vuitton scarves and tug at Prada dresses. Things that in my fantasy will make my days in

Kabul so much simpler, more fun, prettier. The arguments in Naomi Klein's *No Logo* suddenly weigh much lighter than my Eurocard lying on the chrome counter of the boutique. Who says you can't buy happiness? Surely it must be worth a try. I haven't yet experienced a depression that can't be cured with a pair of insanely expensive shoes. It may be a life like a stage set, but at least it's a pretty one.

Putting down my shopping bags, I sit down contentedly at a café to rest for a bit. The buzz of a fan cuts through the air. It isn't long before I'm joined at my table by a man in an impeccable suit and an important expression. He shuffles his papers back and forth on the tabletop, and taps the table with his pen for a minute before he makes his move.

"Are you here on business?" he asks, chewing his lip lightly.

"Not really, more like vacation."

I blow some smoke in his face demonstratively and turn to my magazine again. I think he gets my point. I'm wrong, of course.

"From...?"

He looks encouragingly at me. I look at my well-manicured nails before meeting his eyes.

"From Afghanistan."

His delight knows no bounds.

"Are you an aid worker? How exciting!"

He clasps his hands, as if in prayer.

Oh, you think so? You should see me when loneliness has dug its needle-sharp claws into me. When I open my mouth and don't know what language to start speaking. When I'm sitting in the middle of the junk that makes up my household goods and promise myself not to cry. When I'm tired to the bone of my gypsy existence, and how I depend on the storage and moving company Stadsbuden, with their helpful rolls of packing paper for wrapping everything in. When my curiosity and restlessness feel like a curse and when everything I own has been broken, destroyed, chipped, crushed, or pulverized, along with the feeling of who I am and where I belong. When I wish that all I wanted was a family and a house in the suburbs. When all I want is to pack up one last time.

I smile a fake smile in reply.

"But isn't it dangerous in Afghanistan?"

He looks at me, with an expression of secret understanding. He's moved a little closer now, I'm afraid he'll slide off the edge of his chair.

"Not really," I answer stiffly.

Present fears are less than horrible imaginings.

"But isn't it awful to see all those women in burkas?"

"Sickening."

If it were only a thin blue piece of material that was the problem, and not the fact that half of the population is chained to the ground...

"And how can you stand the poverty?"

"It's hard. Hard to bear."

I'm not the one who has to stand the poverty, you idiot. It's the poor people who must stand it.

I finish my cup of coffee, excuse myself, and retreat with quick steps back to the shops.

Dubai, yet another uneventful vacation day. A sticky heat has beset the country, it's hot as in hell. I go around the city without a plan. I can't even conceal my shallowness by getting theater tickets. But I dutifully go to Dubai Museum and see the homages to Sheikh Rashid Bin Saeed al-Maktoum. He was the father of the current sheikh and the man who laid the foundation for the growth of cosmopolitan Dubai, with the help of oil. The man who replaced a yawning third-world lack of life's necessities with the unbridled excess of the first world. The museum largely consists of arrangements of old objects and manikins depicting life before modernization, a sickening depiction of the traditional and simple life. Room after room filled with picturesque little shops and homes with a folkloric touch, and men – nothing but men everywhere. The text next to the displays describes how after sunset, the nomads would tell stories until the wee hours of the night, eating dried dates. The reconstructed shop stalls remind me of the ones I see in Kabul, but without a dirty carpet of trash and the stench of sewage and desperation. Where is the romance in poverty, illiteracy, and disease? Is there a separate museum for the history of Dubai's women? In any case, that was quite enough cultural veneer for me. I escape out into the sunshine and hop into a taxi, headed for a new shopping center.

My last morning at the hotel. I sit in the breakfast room for a long time, reading and eating – no, overeating, gorging myself on strawberries and pain au chocolat, scrambled eggs, and French cheeses. And even more strawberries. An army of Thai women with stiff hairdos almost invisibly whisk one plate after another from my table. The only place where I've seen Arabian women at work is in the passport control – the rest of the country's female wage workers are Asians, some of the hundreds of thousands of guest workers.

"Another cappuccino, miss?"

I nod encouragingly. No austerity for me.

After breakfast, I check out. I feel ready to return again. My days-long stretch of consumption in the Emirates has managed to puncture my protective cover of resignation and sadness. Now I'm done here, and I'm eager to go back. I have plans to carry out, ideas to test, people to meet, and reports to write. I feel stronger and more optimistic. I board the plane to Kabul, ready to take myself through yet another few months, ready to perfect my selective vision when my gaze comes across the human tatters dressed in rags on the streets.

I can barely carry my heavy bags to the car that's waiting outside the terminal.

"How are things?" I ask routinely as we ride in to town.

Wahab looks worried. He squeezes the wheel with his thin artist hands.

"This situation no good, Miss Diana."

A feeling of guilt grips me.

"What's happened?"

"Yesterday there was a bomb on Jalalabad Road again. Three wounded."

I don't say anything.

"This situation no good, Miss Diana. No good."

The hard rock of unfeeling has suddenly dissolved. My new Miu Miu purse on the seat next to me gnaws uncomfortably at my conscience like some awful crime against humanity. Through the window I see the miserable city pass by, covered in dust and resignation. No, the situation certainly isn't good. It hasn't been good, and probably won't become good in the future either. Through the well-cleaned safety glass, it's always there for inspection, as much as I have the energy for – and even when I no longer have the energy to take it in.

A New Day [June 2005]

It's summer 2005 in Faizabad. For three days, some UN colleagues and I go around to meetings in poky offices with empty desktops in the capital city of the Afghan province Badakhshan. We have meetings at the courthouse, with the prosecutor, with the police chief, and with the governor. There are no computers, no books, no papers, only empty desktops and bucketfuls of green tea.

The only indication of reform that I can see is a swivel chair in the office of the highest judge of the province. The plastic cover is still on it. The judge himself, as he sits in his chair, looks like a religious lunatic in a satire by Parker and Stone, with his long dirty beard and his turban that's as tall as a wedding cake. If countries were ranked by the size of their turbans, Afghanistan would be number one. But as it is, countries are only ranked by income, literacy rates, and welfare, and Afghanistan usually ends up in last place, competing with Sierra Leone and Burkina Faso for the spot. No one can be completely sure, though, because Afghanistan is so poor that its poverty can't be measured, as there aren't any reliable statistics or information. But I've read somewhere that the highest maternal mortality rate ever measured was here in Badakhshan, where 6,500 births out of 100,000 resulted in maternal death. Maybe that's why I don't see any women around.

The judge doesn't shake our hands when we step in. He doesn't even get up. After all, we're just a bunch of women; there isn't a single man in our group except for the interpreter. We sit down on a worn couch in his office. We ask about his background.

"You don't happen to have any education?" we ask carefully.

Yes, he was educated in a madrasa, or Koran school, in Kandahar, during the time when the Taliban movement was growing there. And yes, he's heard about the new constitution. I take that fact as a good sign. It's that kind of day, a day when I try hard to see the good signs. I so want to believe that the future, by definition, brings hope and improvement in its wake, and that I'll be able to squeeze even Badakhshan into my linear progressive world view.

But for each day of our stay, I feel more discouraged. My faith is rocked. I'm not at all sure that there is any future for this corner of Afghanistan. What remains is to persevere in the present.

The car slides through the mud along the narrow main street. There isn't a meter of asphalt in the whole province. There's no power grid and no water either, except for the roaring masses of water in the Kokcha River. The kiosks offer cans of cooking oil, colorful synthetic rope, and pretty kelim saddlebags. A few men trudge through the mud.

"Almost like Strøget," says Marianne, my Danish colleague, referring to the busy shopping street in the heart of Copenhagen.

"Funny, I was thinking exactly the same thing."

A car passes by with three women dressed in burkas. They are sitting perfectly erect in the trunk, whose lid has been removed. From another car, the heads of two dead sheep hang out. They have their mouths open, eyes shut, throats slit.

We are on our way to see Nazir Mohammed, the strongman of the province and yet another of the country's warlords.

During the years that have passed since President Karzai was installed in Kabul, very little has been done to put a stop to all the warlords, the men who tore the country to shreds. They cleaned up their facades with the help of moderate slogans, taking advantage of the western world's distaste for the Taliban as much as possible. They continue to rule in their provinces, they continue to take advantage of the population and spread terror around them. Instead of being held accountable for their actions, or even being marginalized, they've been rewarded with posts as ministers, advisors, police chiefs, and governors.

Nazir Mohammed receives us in a carpeted room without furniture in his gigantic residence, which is still under construction. Nazir Mohammed looks like a classic image of Jesus. He's dressed in a silk robe as white as new snow, with white embroidery, and has medium long, beautifully waved hair. He sits cross-legged on the floor and chooses his words carefully. He talks behind the back of the vice governor, his main rival in the province. It's a mudslinging campaign with heat, emphasis, and energy. Then he washes his hands of it all.

"I want to serve my people," he says, giving yet another example of his plastic relationship to truth. "I live like the people."

Of course, that's nonsense. To live like the people is to barely survive. It's to freeze for half the year, go to bed hungry, not have access to education, information, electricity, healthcare, clean drinking water, or even fifty afghani a day to live on.

"I have no soldiers. What I have is what you see around you."

He gestures around the room, with the hand that wasn't wounded in the war. There is an unmistakable stench of hypocrisy in the air.

"I'm a simple man," he continues.

"Oh, I see," I answer.

I might as well play along in this tragicomedy.

Maybe he's comparing himself to Rabbani, also from Badakhshan. Professor Rabbani is the true alpha male of religious fundamentalism. He was president in the years after the fall of the communist regime and before the Taliban took over, the years during which Kabul was laid to ruin by internal fighting. During the war Rabbani issued his own currency, and with the currency reform, when he was able to exchange the bills he had printed himself for real money, he made a handsome profit. He is now considered to be one of the country's richest people, with property and businesses in the Gulf and Europe. Nowadays he's in Kabul, where he's the party leader for the fundamentalist *Jamiat-e Islami* and part of President Karzai's informal advisory council of Jihadi leaders, that circle of bearded men who bewail every step forward that the country takes and resist it as much as they can. One of my colleagues has compared the effect of the great influence of the warlords in Afghan politics to what it would have been like to build up a democratic post-war Germany with Himmler and Goebbels at the head.

We finish eating our *Kabuli pilaf* and grilled kebab from the plates on the floor. After three hours, it's time to take leave of our host. Nazir Mohammed follows us out, and tells us about the upcoming buzkashi match. Buzkashi is the Afghan variety of polo, where some hundred men, all in a jumble, try to get hold of a goat cadaver while they whip and kick their opponents' horses.

"Don't you want to come and watch?" he asks.

So sorry, unfortunately, we have something else booked.

"But maybe you would at least like to see my buzkashi horses? I have a whole stable full of beautiful buzkashi horses."

So sorry, unfortunately, we must hurry.

Nazir Mohammed remains standing outside his residence, in front of the long line of men who have gathered there and now stand around shuffling their feet in the gravel, waiting to be admitted for an audience. Maybe they want to plead on behalf of a cousin who's been thrown into Nazir Mohammed's private jail, maybe they want to try to regain a piece of confiscated land – who knows. He grips my hand in farewell. Afterwards my palm feels sticky, contaminated.

We meet the representative of the Afghan Independent Human Rights Commission. I squeeze into a place at the table in the Commission's over-furnished office and open up my notebook hopefully. The Commission usually represents a glimmer of hope in the Afghan dusk, a blade of grass to grab hold of. But not here. Its leader heatedly defends the order of things, the hatred of women that is institutionalized in Afghan tradition and culture. He sees the ulema, the group of Islamic scribes who have interpretation rights in religious questions, as a force of good, working hard for women's rights. And he doesn't see anything odd in the fact that a woman can't get a divorce if her husband abuses her. We argue and discuss in an attempt to achieve some kind of recognition of the principle of the equal value of all human beings. We appeal and coax. But to no avail.

"It's against our culture," he says and smiles, a smile that smooths things over and that makes me want to knock his teeth out.

"But your culture is crap."

No, I don't say that. I only think it. I only mean it.

"In Afghanistan we respect our women," he explains with a satin smooth voice, while his eyes inspect me as if I deserve twenty years of hard labor.

The same old tune, like a scratched 78 record. A mantra that can't be elaborated or explained. And then the three lone women in the Afghan government are held up as an example, like a constant alibi for the ruthlessness of the patriarchy. The presence of these three women – a women's minister, a youth minister, and a minister for martyrs – is supposed to compensate for the hair-raising crimes that are quietly committed against Afghan women in the name of religion, or culture, or both mixed together.

It becomes harder and harder for all of us to conceal our irritation. His female colleague steps in and tries to smooth over the situation.

"Here in Afghanistan, women have the privilege of always being protected. They are always protected by their husband and their family. They are never alone."

But who protects her from her husband and family? I want to ask. Not tradition, not the law, not Allah. Instead I give up.

Why don't the oppressed go on strike? Why don't the hungry steal? The only thing the rulers have managed to achieve is a shard of hell. But how are the Afghan women to know that? Everything in their lives is controlled, except for the content of truth in the air. In the car as we leave, I dream of millions of angry Moslem women who settle their accounts with the ruling interpretation of Islam. I dream of flying over the whole country dropping leaflets with Valerie Solanas' SCUM Manifesto in Persian translation. But then it occurs to me that almost no one can read, and the steam goes out of me. I exhale with a long, faint hiss, like when someone sticks a knife into a beach ball.

We meet the newly appointed governor, an elderly man who reminds me of some maharaja from *Arabian Nights*. A Pashtun in Tajik enemy country. He squints at me from under his turban when I ask him how the economy of the province can get on its feet.

"Apples," he answers.

Apples are going to rescue the province.

"No other apples are as good as the ones from Badakhshan."

He tugs dreamily at his white beard.

"For a kilo of apples, you can get twelve afghani," he explains.

That's about twenty cents.

As I leave the governor's building, I take a look around. It says "Governery" on the sign above the gate. Clouds with multilayered flounces decorate the sky. We drive back through the city on the muddy, potholed road past the mud houses. It's a ghastly place. I wonder how many kilos of apples they would need to achieve even a little bit of prosperity here. And there are mountains all around, mountains everywhere. There isn't even one little windswept apple tree in sight.

SUMMER

Vacation. I have dutifully, at their request, made an appointment at the MFA in order to report to the personnel department. "My" staff advisor, a woman of about my own age, leads the conversation. She's a human resources specialist and recruits MFA employees to our embassies in Asia.

"How many of you are there at the office? Where do you live? Did you bring a car with you?"

I try not to show my surprise at the fact that she knows absolutely nothing about the situation, or the conditions in the countries to which she is responsible for sending people. What should an HR specialist be expected to know, if not something about the staff, their jobs, and their working conditions? I'm sitting on one side of her messy desk, and we're drinking coffee. I wish I hadn't come. I could have pretended that I never saw the telegram asking me to come here – considering the bad communications, that would have been very believable. The sun is out, and I would rather meet my friends than sit here and talk to someone who so obviously isn't listening anyway. Nonetheless, I give her the basic course on Afghanistan. Patiently I tell her about the security situation, the standard of living, the cooperation with Sida staff, the lack of communication, that no insurance company in the universe would want to insure my car if I bought one and drove it there, and that car driving for women is not recommended.

"And how often do you travel to Istanbul?"

"Istanbul?"

The last time I was there? It must have been the summer of 1991.

"You mean Islamabad?"

"Oh, yes, Islamabad. OK."

She shrugs. Same thing, more or less.

"And what's it like to work there, as a woman?"

In Istanbul? Or in Islamabad?! No, that's it for me.

A few minutes later, I've escaped out to the street in a shower of excuses. I walk along Malmskillnadsgatan down toward Sergels

Torg and don't know whether to laugh or cry. Or just buy her an atlas.

POOR PEOPLE DON'T NEED ANY ART
[AUGUST 2005]

The Roof of Bamiyan Hotel is said to be owned by the former governor's wife, who rents it out to Vice President Khalili's brother. It's a modest, rundown one-story house with wall to wall carpets that are too big, and shabby rooms without a toilet. The beds are too short, and have worn out blankets and threadbare sheets – you couldn't get any further than this from the soulless furnishings of the corporate hotel factory. But the view from the plateau where the house stands is magnificent. From here you can see the valley's poplars, green fields, and willow trees, and the cliff where Bamiyan's famous pair of Buddha statues stood for almost two thousand years, until the Taliban blew them up in March 2001. The two empty niches in the golden brown rock look like two gaps in a row of teeth.

Bamiyan lies in the Afghan central massive, part of Hindu Kush. It takes more than ten hours to get here by car from Kabul, or twenty minutes by plane. The population is dominated by Hazara, the Mongolian people who, according to legend, are descendants of Genghis Khan. The Hazara have always been at the bottom of the Afghan social pecking order, feared, oppressed, persecuted, and poor.

I'm sitting outside in the gravel-covered yard with Mariko, my Dutch friend and colleague, drinking wine that we've brought with us and comparing our impressions from the day. It's evening and there's a full moon. The neon lights of the hotel shine green and yellow. The valley is lush. I haven't seen so much green in one place since I came to this godforsaken land, with its thick-skinned, unbelievably tenacious people. On the other side, the cliff with its Buddha holes glows in the dark, as if Allah had mounted a large flashlight behind the mountain.

We are joined in the yard by Baqer Moin, a BBC journalist who has been reporting from Iran and Afghanistan for twenty years and who is also staying at the hotel. He talks to us about some Afghan female postmodern poets he's met.

"The Pashtun have no tradition of questioning their own culture. All attempts at modernization today come from outside of the society, not inside," he explains, puffing at his cigarillo. "But these poets represent something absolutely unique!"

His enthusiasm makes hope return for a second; the thin mountain air feels more breathable again.

But most of all Baqer Moin talks about himself.

"Everyone here knows who I am. Everyone!"

He lights yet another cigarillo and slowly exhales the smoke in front of him. It can't conceal his self-satisfied air.

"The hotel proprietor couldn't believe his eyes when I checked in. 'Baqer Moin!' he cried, gaping. 'Welcome!'"

The next day we're invited to dinner at the home of Kamal, who works for the World Health Organization. We bump along through the valley in a Mercedes Geländewagen, to the tones of Leyla Forouhar, passing little mud houses with neat woodpiles and piles of cow patties. Out on the fields, the farmers and their oxen are struggling with this year's potato harvest. Sinewy donkeys are grazing in the ditches at the side of the fields. Dirty children are playing in the dust; the game seems to consist of the bigger ones hitting the smaller ones. The breath of globalization hasn't wafted this far, except in the guise of an occasional Toyota pick-up truck or satellite phone.

The guests are already there when we arrive. There are a few UN employees, and aid workers wearing scarves and shabby clothes, who are sitting on a carpet with their plates in front of them on the floor. Trés ethno-chic. The discussion soon turns to the destroyed buddhas. A few weeks ago, the artist Hiro Yamagata presented a proposal for a project to celebrate the memory of the statues. Using a laser system, he would project 140 overlapping, faceless statues in neon green, pink, white, orange, and blue onto the cliff and the niches where the statues once stood, for a few hours every Sunday evening. Each image would continuously change pattern and color, and the projectors would be powered by about forty wind turbines, since Bamiyan almost completely lacks electric power. The whole thing would cost eight million dollars, partly sponsor money from Mercedes-Benz. The suggestion was met with cautious optimism by Afghan representatives, who left the final decision to the UN body UNESCO. But UNESCO's goodwill ambassador, Ikuo Hirayama, objected that it would be better to leave the holes in the cliff wall as they are, as a symbol of humanity's barbarism.

I think about Baqer Moin's argument that culture is the driving engine of society. It seems to me that I see humanity's barbarism symbolized everywhere. I would like to see a few laser buddhas instead, for a change.

"An incredibly cool idea," I exclaim.

I hear weak sighs and groans from around the rug, where Yamagata's laser show seems to be about as popular as malaria.

"But can't you at least see the irony in the Buddha statues being reincarnated using lasers? After all, the Taliban opposed everything that might be considered modern."

A short but painful silence.

"But it doesn't fit in here," objects a tanned, pumped up New Zealander with teeth as white as lumps of sugar.

He reminds me of someone from a surfing video. I can't help wondering if you can buy teeth like that, and if so, where. I can't help but want to squeeze those upper arms a little.

"But who would come here and see it?" asks Stacy, one of the girls with an embroidered shawl draped around her shoulders and big wooden jewelry – very Bohemian chic.

Tourists? No, hardly in any significant numbers. It appears that that idea was already suggested more than forty years ago by Jan Myrdal in his book *Travels in Afghanistan*, and look what happened. Then, in 1959, Myrdal was in Bamiyan, dreaming of brotherhood between peoples and ambitious tourism projects. He predicted that Afghanistan would become one of Asia's great tourist countries. He was wrong, of course, about Afghanistan as well as everything else. A wave of opium-smoking hippies in the 1960s and 1970s found their way here, but otherwise tourists have preferred more carefree places through the years.

"People who live in Bamiyan? People like you and me?"

Stacy snorts.

"But why? What use would it be?"

Use? Isn't it enough that it's art? I make an attempt to defend my newfound, unexpected, and unconsidered position as agitator for the free arts.

"L'art pour l'art?"

Both my French and Gautier's art theories are completely wasted on Stacy, Surfboy, and the others. Stacy looks at me with distaste.

"But they don't even have water or electricity here," she says.

The arguments remind me of the county council debates at home. Why must the cost of culture always be weighed against the cost of healthcare? Why is it never weighed against the travel budget for municipal officials? Or a tax increase? Or the state's purchase of advanced weapon systems? The draft? Building roads? Support of the press?

Stacy, and the flock on the rug around her, look at me with condescension – no, with contempt. I wonder if they really think that Mercedes-Benz and Yamagata are going to shell out eight million dollars for a water project if there isn't be any laser show. As I see it, the choice is between Bamiyan with a laser show but no electricity or water, or Bamiyan without a laser show, electricity, or water.

Kandahar II [September 2005]

It's the middle of September, a few days before the parliamentary elections. I'm sitting in a container, listening to the military version of what's happening in the southern parts of the country, what's happening with the insane "GWOT", the unpromising global war against terror. War on terrorists is a concept that I can understand, but war on terror? A war on terrorism? How can you combat a feeling, or a method? And beyond these nebulous slogans, people forget all the other things that are necessary to stop the spread of extremism: food, jobs, laws that are followed, education. They forget the masses of alienated, angry, unemployed young men who dream of change and a future that never comes. The asymmetry never ceases to fascinate me – the blinding high-tech war machine of the coalition forces against the low-tech men with their Kalashnikov replicas, barefoot and with tangled beards. But a fistful of gravel will go a long way, if you just manage to poke it right down into the oiled machinery. My thoughts are interrupted when a young major strides in through the door, straight-backed, with a spring in his step, and joins us.

"Here's the real expert on the Uruzgan Province," explains Colonel Vollrath, chief of the Dutch Special Forces at Kandahar's airport.

He points to the American next to him. The major has been in the country for one year. He's blond and muscular, and looks like a baseball hero in some saccharine college movie. He tells us about how the Americans in Uruzgan have "face to face contact" with Uruzgan residents. It sounds silly. Face to face contact. Yes, what else are you supposed to do if you think you're here to win their hearts? Shout through a megaphone from a Humvee, the monstrous armored cars that they insist on driving around in? Bomb the villages with halal-prepared Happy Meals? At the same time, I don't blame him. I wouldn't agree to travel to Uruzgan even if someone threatened me at gunpoint. Uruzgan is too dangerous for my taste. I may be adventurous, but I don't have a death wish, at least not right now.

"Have you heard anything about Mazdaria, and the claims that he runs his election campaign from Governor Jan Mohammed's office?" Tomas, my travel companion from the German embassy, asks the major.

Tomas knows everything. He knows everything and everyone. He speaks Pashto and Dari and has been in the country at various times since the 1980s, beginning with a stint as an East German diplomat. He's one of a handful of Westerners who have at least come close to understanding the Afghan riddle.

A look of uncertainty sweeps over the major.

"I'm not sure I know who Mazdaria is."

A scent of cologne wafts out when he shifts his weight in the simple folding chair.

"He's one of the main candidates in Uruzgan," says Tomas.

He has suddenly lost all interest in staying there or listening.

After the meeting, we drive back to town along the desolate road. There's nothing but desert around us in all directions. A forty-degree hot wind blows through the open car window. Tomas doesn't have much use for military people in general, and I don't think our latest meeting has helped convince him that the international military presence here will ever steer the country in the right course. Or the presence of any of us, for that matter. But he doesn't say anything; I'm only surmising. And I share his doubts. After the Taliban were driven from power there was no grand strategy for how the building of this state should come about. The united international community is no better than this. Under different circumstances it might be more effective, but not as things are now. Afghanistan is like a leaky boat that we're all sitting in. Instead of stopping up the holes where the leaks have sprung, we just scoop out water and boast about how many scoops we've emptied, how many bails we've contributed, and how big they are.

We sit in the back seat and look out over the hot landscape, and a few camels who are walking by in the sand. After the lecture we've had about all the IEDs, or improvised explosive devices, in the province, I'm scanning the side of the road for suspicious objects. That oil drum maybe? Or that broken moped? No. It's no use, there's nothing I can do with the information except get more frightened. Or lock myself in somewhere, join the bunker people. But I don't feel like doing either of those. I'm thinking about something else. From the stereo we hear Coldplay's *Talk*, which Tomas and I quickly started calling the Taliban song.

> *Are you lost or incomplete?*
> *Do you feel like a puzzle, you can't find your missing piece?*
> *Tell me, how do you feel?*
> *Well, I feel like they're talking in a language I don't speak*
> *And they're talking it to me*[3]

An over-produced song takes on new dimensions.

We meet Mullah Khaksar, who was chief of the intelligence service and after that, deputy minister of the interior responsible for security under the Taliban regime. Now he's been pardoned and is a candidate in the parliamentary election.

Mullah Khaksar is sitting in an armchair drinking tea and watching football on what the Taliban used to call the "devil's box" when we enter. We sit down in the bare room. Mullah Khaksar switches the channel to Tolo TV and its music program, which is playing upbeat techno. Almost reluctantly, he lowers the volume a tiny, tiny bit, so that he can hear what we're saying.

Mullah Khaksar lights a Pine cigarette and offers us Pepsi-Cola and nuts. We talk about the election campaign and Khaksar's own candidacy. We talk about the reconciliation process and Khaksar's own ambitions to form a party; a large, national, cross-ethnic party. He wants change, he says. He thinks that women have a place in society. That's why he left the Taliban, he tells us.

---

3   Coldplay, "Talk." *X&Y*, Capitol, 2005. *Genius, genius.com/Coldplay-talk-lyrics.*

"So what do you want to do if you're elected? What issues do you plan to work on?"

Mullah Khaksar looks at us uncomprehendingly. He doesn't understand the question at all.

The power goes out. The music dies out. For a moment we remain sitting in the dark, talking about election fraud.

The next day we meet Noor-ul-haq Olomi, once prominent in the old communist regime, now a party leader and one of the stronger candidates for a place in parliament. Olomi dreams that his new party will be large, national, and cross-ethnic.

"We want change," he says, offering us Super Cola and nuts. "We must be nice to each other," says Olomi.

He repeats that again and again, and again. How people should be nice to each other in Afghanistan. Finally we take our leave.

We meet Qayum Karzai, the president's brother, who is also a candidate in the parliamentary election. Qayum is a copy of his brother the president. He sits in the same way, speaks the same way, laughs as often, gestures in the same way. He's charming and well-spoken. We mostly talk about the upcoming election. Qayum is sure of victory.

"Oh dear, how will this all turn out?" he complains with satisfaction. "For the first time in my life I have to arrange my own move, buy furniture, and find somewhere to live in Kabul."

He doesn't even seem to reflect on the unpredictability of the election system, or the fact that many others besides him are competing for the positions. Maybe he has good reason not to.

President Karzai has refused to take the lead in any party or block. He blames it on the fact that he hates political parties, and argues that it was the growth of political parties that laid the country in ruins. But at heart there is also an awareness that a party or a movement led by him would be a Pashtun party rather than a multi-ethnic and national one. And, what's worse, there is frustration with Karzai even among the ranks of the Pashtuns themselves. There's growing dissatisfaction in the Pashtun belt along the Afghan-Pakistani border, where the war against terrorism is being waged and at the same time, aid efforts cannot reach their target because of the ever worsening security situation. For centuries, rivalries between different Pashtun clans have been more important than religion, political ideology, and everything in between, and many Pashtuns don't see the cosmopolitan and educated Karzai as a real Pashtun. There's a risk that this will result in a split parliament that the President can neither control nor confront with any great success.

During our conversation, Ahmed Wali, another one of the president's brothers, slips into the room. He is considered by many to be one of Afghanistan's most powerful drug kings. Ahmed Wali is barefoot and dressed in shalwar kamiz. He looks a bit shy. He drinks tea, fidgeting with his toes, and follows the discussion with interest, although he doesn't say much. Ahmed Wali is a candidate as well, but for the toothless and powerless provincial council.

"If he doesn't stay in Kandahar he can't keep track of his drug empire," a colleague remarks sarcastically.

Yes, and what would happen then? Drug money lubricates just about every cog in the Afghan economy.

Before we go, Qayum invites us to dinner that evening. We are about ten people. We eat pilaf, chicken, and vegetables, and for three hours we analyze the actions of the world community, the Afghans' own responsibility, the building of institutions, and what should be done next. There are only two questions we never really take up: the result of the president's work and the anti-drug campaign.

"We want change," says Qayum.

Maybe you should talk to your brother about that, I think to myself.

The next evening we're invited to dinner by the governor, Haji Asadullah. He's 34 years old and has a violent, bloody past as a Mujahedin closely allied with Abdul Rasul Sayyaf and his fundamentalist party Ittehad-e Islami.

Sayyaf is not just an Islamic law professor. If you didn't know better, he could be taken for an old man in a fairytale, with his white clothes and his long white beard. Or one of the wise men. He's urbane, well-traveled, well-read, and owns property. But beneath the pious surface, he is one of the country's most hard driving political and religious actors, and the incarnation of Islamic fundamentalism of the Wahabi strain in Afghanistan. In the early 1990s, Sayyaf sponsored several of the terrorist camps in Afghanistan and Pakistan. Unsurprisingly, he is also one of the candidates in the upcoming parliamentary election, in the Paghman District outside Kabul.

But Sayyaf feels far away when Haji Azadullah receives us in the private part of his residence on this warmish evening.

The governor is dressed in a tennis sweater and sneakers, and sports a ten-day growth of beard. He is relaxed and charismatic; he reminds me of a more brutal version of the Serbian cello teacher I once studied with (and liked very much). Azadullah flops down on the couch next to me, draping his arm along the backrest behind me. Tomas and I exchange glances. It's a good thing that my family isn't from these parts, that could have been unpleasant.

"We want to have change," says the governor in good English. "It's time for a new generation to take over," he says, leaning confidentially in my direction.

Maybe you should talk to Sayyaf about that, I think, moving discreetly a little further toward the front edge of the couch.

Qayum too attends the dinner. He's accompanied by his uncle, a sweet old gentleman who is Afghanistan's ambassador in the Czech Republic. Before dinner we talk about what the UN's role should be in Afghanistan now, once the elections are over and the Bonn Agreement draws to an end.

"The UN, yes, what should the UN do?" says the ambassador with a contagious laugh. "The UN is like a respectable old grandfather who's in the hospital on life support. If you pull out the plug he'll die. But of course no one wants to kill old grandfather, whom everyone respects so much. Instead you go there with flowers every single day, ask how he's doing, fuss over him a little and show your great respect."

He laughs.

"But to imagine that Grandfather is going to do something – no, I don't think we should do that."

I wonder pessimistically if Afghanistan is going to meet the same fate as the UN.

It's long past curfew time when we drive back to the UN guest house where we're staying. For safety's sake, the governor sends a jeep packed full of soldiers to escort us through the desolate city.

Election day. It's a hot day – how else could it be in the desert in the middle of September? Through the car window the landscape sweeps by, simple and stripped down, and far removed from the commercialism that I assumed for so long to be the natural state of things. I'm sitting in the breeze from the open window and feel that today the sun is in the sky for my sake. Here I come, sailing through life, before the wind.

The air is vibrating with heat, and I'm vibrating a little from the excitement. How simple it is to equate election and democracy! To push away all the other necessary conditions, at least for a moment, if nothing else then to not seem so sour and negative. Democracy Afghan Style, its veneer thin as gold leaf.

Tomas and I are driving through the boarded up, desolate streets of the Daman District east of the city of Kandahar. With us we have Huma, my interpreter. I'm thankful that I've found her, through Tomas' many contacts.

The women who are allowed to work are a pathetically small group, and for a long time I didn't dare think it was true that Huma could work with us. But at the last minute she received permission from her family to go, and the day before the election she turned up in Kandahar to meet me.

At every election center we split up. Tomas goes to the male election halls, Huma and I visit the female ones, relegated to someone's home or squeezed into the smallest classroom of a school.

Huma is a fantastic interpreter. She speaks excellent English. She's enthusiastic, smart, and alert, and moves around in the election places like a police officer at a crime scene. Her very being makes me happy, ignites a faint hope that Afghanistan's young generation of women might be allowed to experience a different future than their mothers. The country needs its women, like a bird needs both of its wings.

"I want to be a criminal investigator," she says when I ask what her plans are after university.

I think she's been watching too much CSI.

"You would be an excellent investigator."

Not that I know the first thing about police work, but I really mean it. Huma chews bubblegum and looks around, wide-eyed. Except for the time when her family was exiled and living in Quetta, she has never been outside of Kabul.

We drive from one voting place to another. We are offered Zam-Zam Cola and nuts. It's calm, almost soporific, and sadly few women voters are out.

The next day we eat a final breakfast – omelette or fried eggs? – at the guesthouse before flying back to Kabul. While we're waiting to board the UN plane, a small, unpiloted, windowless spy plane lands on the runway and rolls toward us. Otherwise the journey is uneventful.

Three days later Tomas calls.

"Huma called and she was crying. Her father is angry with her because she was seen with a foreign man during the trip."

He sounds so grim that I can barely understand what he's saying.

"He says that she's brought shame and dishonor on the family, and he's not going to let her continue at the university," he continues.

According to *pashtunwali*, the Pashtun code of honor, the family's honor is more important than everything else. It makes no difference whether it's a sheep theft or a daughter who's been dishonored in some way; honor must be defended at any price.

We decide to go to Microrayon right away, the pallid, Stasi-gray complex of dilapidated rental buildings where she lives. These are the same modular concrete buildings that are found in the suburbs of Kiev, Yerevan, and Tallinn. They must be that shabby and ugly on purpose. There must be a sick brain behind it, a Dr. Mengele of architecture, obsessed with the idea of making people's lives as unendurable as possible.

Huma has been beaten so badly that she can hardly stand up when she meets us. Wincing, she sinks down shakily onto a pillow in the depressing living room of the depressing apartment. We sit down with her father's brother, Dr. Saber, to drink tea.

Dr. Saber is furious with his brother and waves his arms around angrily.

"How can he do this? He's a member of the Democratic Party! He says he wants change in Afghanistan! And he doesn't think twice about going to Germany and drinking beer!"

He talks at a staccato pace, drawing in breath and new rage after every sentence.

"And then he treats his daughter like this!"

"He says I've brought shame on the family," Huma interjects.

"Thatanythingcouldhavehappenedandnoonewillwant tomarryme."

She fights back tears.

"ButIhaven'tdoneanythingwrongnothinghappened!"

"I don't want my sister's daughter to marry a man who thinks along those lines," says Saber.

He rocks back and forth on the pillow where he's sitting.

"My brother is crazy! How will we ever achieve change in this country! I'll throw him out of the party! The Democratic Party!"

Saber shakes his head, and buries his face in his hands for a moment. Tomas looks angry. He demands time and again to get to meet the brother and hear from his own mouth that he, Tomas, his friend from years back, isn't good enough to be *maharam*, chaperone, for his daughter. I listen to the heated exchange about Reputation and Honor. It feels like I've been moved a few centuries back and landed in a Pushkin novel, right before the duel, with Tomas as principal and Dr. Saber as his second.

I feel more depressed than I have in a long time. The dizzying one billion that we just put into the election, and all the solemn talk about change and democracy in Afghanistan – is the result no more than a pleasant illusion? All the beautiful words break so easily against hard realities. Aside from the fact that the country's figureheads have learned a few empty phrases about democracy and respect for women's rights, things are mostly just the way they've always been. The election is not really part of a broader process of institution-building or democratization. And what are all the conventions and laws about women enjoying the same rights as men, if not a mockery, a few papers to wave around in order to satisfy aid donors? For the people of Afghanistan, the Taliban's fall from power hasn't calibrated any new ground zero, not for the women, and not for anyone else. It's only one more regime that has been toppled, one in a long line. The massive international presence in the country – cadres of eager, good-hearted aid workers, military personnel, and diplomats – is no more than an aside in the bloody, brutal history of Afghanistan.

I look at Huma; her eyes are shiny with tears and fixed on the rug. She looks crushed, a different person from the one I let out of the car outside the gate just a few days earlier. Like a bird with only one wing.

Islamabad [October 2005]

It's Thursday morning and I'm taking a UN plane to Islamabad, my main breathing hole. I spend two days at the embassy reading all the reports that can't reach me in Kabul, and sending the reports that I've written but can't send from there, since the office has no secure means of communication. The Swedish military effort in Afghanistan costs about 35 million dollars per year. In 2004, 44 million were earmarked for aid. For the political leg of our engagement, however – one (1) diplomat on site – there aren't even enough resources to equip me with a secure means of communication. Or a computer with an internet connection that works the way it should.

At some point during my first few months, I sent a report home to the Ministry about the importance of being able to communicate like this in the 2000s. It was an official request, with case number and everything, just in case the managers at headquarters had forgotten or happened to overlook this detail. Since then, I've badgered and argued. The ambassador has badgered and argued. No reaction. When I left Afghanistan, almost two years later, we still had not received any answer. The bureaucrats back there in Stockholm who plan, organize, and budget, who decide how thick the walls of the archive should be, which office furniture should be bought on behalf of the government office, and whether I or someone else needs a trip per year in order to rest up a little, or maybe three – these people are always out of step with the rest of the MFA's activity. Sometimes there are such huge gaps between the political ambitions, the field, and the Excel spreadsheets that an official without communication easily falls through the gaps. Only to suddenly flicker up on a screen somewhere in the bureaucracy.

In any case, without a secure means of communication, I have a reason to go to Islamabad as often as I have the time for it. And the lack of information that reaches me from the outside world via my computer and inbox gives me the best excuse in the world to stay out of the office. Instead I can meet people, investigate by myself, reach my own conclusions.

I enjoy what seems like an easy and worry-free existence in the Pakistani capital, compared to Afghanistan. It's an illusion – Pakistan is probably the world's most dangerous country, with its nuclear weapons, Islamic extremists, and unsolved conflicts; both a victim and a sponsor of terrorism. Nonetheless, it works for a few days. Visually it looks like a normal city – a modernist creation with rectangular city blocks and neat flower beds, shopping centers, and cars with license plates. During the day, I sit in the embassy. In the evening I go and get a massage, then I sit curled up in a sofa at the residence drinking wine or tea with the ambassador. We laugh at the foolishness of the world, vent our frustrations. And I go swimming. The pool is deserted, and it's heavenly.

On Sunday morning I take the plane back. On board with me I have a shopping bag filled with pirated DVDs to watch during lonely evenings in Kabul, and canned German pumpernickel. A new week can begin.

Inspection [November 2005]

I don't know how many times I've gone to Islamabad already, but this time it's not a welcome interruption; I only feel irritated. One of the MFA's inspectors is visiting Islamabad. On behalf of our employer, he is supposed to inspect whether the embassy's activities are in order, and make sure that things are done according to all kinds of rule books and regulations. Yet he and his colleague have cancelled their visit to Kabul at the last minute. It's too dangerous. If my friends don't dare to come here, I can more or less understand it, but my employer? The same employer who doesn't want to pay for more armored cars for the office? Who usually meet reports of the ever-worsening security situation with silence? If my Sida colleagues and I can be here month after month, then how can it be too dangerous for Mr. Inspector to come for two days? Swallowing my contempt, I fly to Pakistan.

The inspector is a slow, heavy-set man, who mostly seems interested in the golf tour he's worked into the program now that the cancelled trip to Kabul has given him some extra time. We spend an hour or so talking about what the work situation is like in Afghanistan. He lectures us all about various regulations, he strews platitudes and meaningless remarks around, he asks questions that all bear the unmistakable mark of ignorance. Not for a minute do I let him forget that he didn't dare go there himself. I do everything except openly mock him, even though I'm tempted.

I'm on the United Nations plane on my way back. If only the UN Humanitarian Assistance Support, which shuttles between the world's war zones, had a rewards program, I could have scraped together enough for a free trip to Abéché or Basra by now! Still, I love the short flight over the breathtakingly beautiful mountains.

Lost in Translation
[December 2005]

Christmas is approaching. Ever since October I've been dreading it. Christmas in Kabul is out of the question. That would be like an invitation to self-pity, and I've had enough of that. But I don't want to go home, I'm afraid to open up all the old wounds. As long as I'm here – or anywhere else, but away from Stockholm – I feel safe. Christmas has never been my favorite – nor any other holiday either, for that matter. It becomes so palpable that I don't really feel at home. So much more pleasant then to stay away, to choose to be a stranger among strangers instead. In other places, I can bear my self-imposed alienation with a straight back, it's a role that I can easily shoulder.

I examine my choices. I've had an overload of new impressions, I don't want to see anything new. I don't want to know anything, or learn anything. I just want to rest my senses for a while. If it were possible to travel to a white room covered in cotton I would do it. Maybe an insane asylum...

I settle on a trip to Tokyo, where my sister Helga is studying Japanese. I promise myself to see as little as possible, not rush around, just take it easy.

When I arrive, Helga's classes are still in session. For the first two days, I mainly sit with my laptop in the room that I've rented in her student dormitory. Or I lie stretched out on the bed, with my nose in a book. And I sleep, a lot. Deeply and without dreams – no strange dreams that I'm killing people, that my friends are lying buried under rubble, or that Kabul is in flames. After a few days, when I've grown tired of this, I go out on the town by myself, surrounded by a chaos of foreign characters. I drift around with my mind at peace. I smile at the well-swept streets; at the straight lines that people form when waiting for the metro, which stops so that the doors line up exactly with the markings on the platform; at the bowing, attractive shop attendants who greet me with doll-like faces and soft voices. I smile at the odd translations on the signs. At the toilets, with their warmed seats and their built-in control panels with as many buttons as a reactor station. I feel like I've landed in paradise.

I find Tobu, a department store as big as a small Swedish town, where I can instinctively navigate without too much trouble. It's a female genetic capability, unresearched by science. Everywhere there are smiling, bowing salespeople. I buy a skirt, too short to be usable, but I want it anyway.

The salesperson spends forever folding it.

Wrapping it in the rustling tissue paper.

Fastening it with a golden sticker label.

Tying a pretty ribbon around the package.

Opening up a shopping bag made of the thickest, glossiest paper.

Placing the package in the bottom of the bag.

Tying the bag with a thick satin ribbon.

Folding the receipt in half, edge to edge.

Placing it in a pretty envelope in pressed linen.

Laying the little envelope on a silver plate.

Handing me the plate with both hands.

I feel like a prize racehorse as I stand there shifting from foot to foot, eyes wide open, dumbfounded.

She carries the bag to the exit for me.

Hands it to me.

Nods.

Bows.

With the bag in my hand, I sink into a chair at one of the cafes in the department store. To be in the land of 120 percent is stressful too, in its own particular way. All this precision makes me feel tired and excited at the same time. I love it, and I hate it. It's like living life through a magnifying glass. No detail is too small, nothing is irrelevant.

When the waitress appears with a winsome smile, I order coffee and point to a piece of cake among the colorful pictures in the menu. She clasps her hands and bows lightly before steering herself backwards from my table. She soon returns.

The waitress shows me the cake.

Wipes the knife.

Makes an incision worthy of a surgeon.

Carefully pulls the knife up again.

Wipes it with care.

Makes a new cut, sculpting an aesthetically proportioned piece.

She wipes off the knife.

Exchanges it for a clean cake server.

Carefully works the server in under the cake.

Puts it on a plate.

Places a small fork next to it.

Sets down the plate in front of me with a bow.

A few days pass by, pleasantly, easily, and without friction.

Then the spell is broken. The day before Christmas, my grandmother passes away. My sweet little grandmother, thin as a leaf, gone. It didn't happen suddenly, but – now she's gone.

All the visits that I didn't get around to, all the conversations where I had so little to say, all the postcards I never wrote – they now ram through my heart like a samurai sword.

Far down in the twisted corridors of my brain, I've stored away my picture of her, afraid to summon it up too often, for fear that it will get worn out. The picture of Grandmother, who taught me how to bake Finnish cookies and coffee bread in her apartment in Umeå one long-ago summer. Grandmother, who would take me to the swimming place by the sea where the water is barely twelve degrees Celsius, and I would get out of the water frozen blue, happy. Grandmother, who had never been out of the country, but who talked about how she and I would someday take the ferry across to Vasa in Finland over there someplace on the other side of the Gulf of Bothnia, and discover the world.

Grandmother, who in her final years only talked about Russia. In the fog of her old age, geography and concepts had grown dim.

"What are you going to do in Russia?" she laughed the last time we met.

"Afghanistan, Grandma. Afghanistan! It's been several years now since I moved from Moscow."

"And Russia is so dangerous, too. Oh, my goodness, how awful!"

And then her contagious laugh again.

On her dresser, there's a picture of me curtsying and greeting the Queen during a state visit to Moscow. Maybe that's where her sense of time stopped, as far as I was concerned. In Grandmother's world, nothing could be finer than this royalist glow. Just think, I actually met the royal couple! How wonderful.

Which one of us is most alone? She travels alone to that place, wherever it may be, if it exists at all – to the hidden valley of eternity. And I'm left alone in the land of the living, with all those things I wanted to tell her.

A New Beginning [January 2006]

I'm back in Kabul after Christmas, and it feels so good. It's good to be away, but best of all to be at home. In lambskin slippers and three layers of pashmina shawls, I shuffle around in my house, feeling cozy. The generator is on around the clock now; it sounds like there's a tractor in the garden that keeps running and running. But it's warm, it must be 20 degrees on the first floor, at least if I also turn on my gas heater. And I love that it is a new year – a new year that will be better.

Once I'm back in the office, I read a copy of the inspection report that's arrived. In the very stiffest office Swedish, the inspector notes in passing that the security situation in Kabul is exposed. And then he recommends that the embassy in Islamabad should carry out a fire drill. A fire drill! I laugh for a whole week.

Everyday Life in Kabul

The darkness is dense, the air cold. I'm walking from the gym at ISAF's headquarters toward the gate. I'm still sweaty but excited, pumped up with endorphines. Kabir is waiting outside the gate; as an Afghan he's not allowed to drive in to the area. How strange it seems to me that they never read, I think to myself, as so often before when I've kept one of our drivers waiting behind the wheel for way too long. They don't read a magazine or a book, or listen to the radio, or do anything but just sit there, staring out in the darkness. All this inactivity makes me feel stressed, as if I'm wasting their lives.

Kabir drives to my home past the American embassy. The block around it is closed off but when you're in a car with diplomatic plates you can pass through the barriers and snake around the sandbags and the oil drums in a zigzag out to the other side.

An American contractor, about 35, meets us as we slow down at the first barrier.

"Why didn't you switch off the headlights?" the man hisses to Kabir when he rolls down the window to show his ID card.

He has long, wavy hair under a cap, and his finger is on the trigger of his automatic weapon. He's an employee of one of the many private security companies that have sprung up, companies to whom states now delegate certain parts of the violence monopoly with a shrug of the shoulders.

"But I did, sir," says Kabir.

"Not fast enough!"

Kabir smiles in reply. He always smiles.

"Next time I will have to shoot you."

All at once my good mood has evaporated. *To win hearts and minds.* Indeed.

"What a jerk," I say as we drive on. "This is your country, not his."

"He was not very polite," Kabir says cheerfully.

When will he and all the others finally be fed up? What is this cynical trash doing here in the first place? They would never have found employment at home, but here they can play king and make a fortune guarding a roadblock. I want to throw myself out of the car and run back to that bastard, tell him that this is Kabir's country, Kabir's streets, Kabir's dignity. Then let him shoot me if he feels like it.

But we have already stopped outside my gate. I say goodnight and go inside, my hand balled up in an angry fist inside my pocket.

Worlds Apart

Nick is going to play records at Samarkand, and I've promised to be there. The place is full of people. It's like being in a gay club; most of the clientele are men who spend way more time than average at the gym. Postmodern nomads who can live in a trench for months if necessary. Tough, wonderful, fantastic people. Cynical, disillusioned, arrogant people. People who, like me, have a vain wish to make a difference, but maybe don't believe that they are. Save the world or die trying.

I've never liked Samarkand, the new "in" place, but it's the happening of the month. On the ground floor there's a restaurant serving vapid and greasy central Asian food. On the second floor, a long bar stretches out, big as a lounge. Every time I pass through the door, I reflect that if I were the Taliban I would choose exactly this place to attack. It's near the street, filled with westerners, zero security planning (many of the guests have brought their own weapons that they can brandish on the way home after too much alcohol), a nest of sin. There would be a car with explosives, straight through the entryway – boom, finished. And every time, I push the thought aside. It's no use worrying.

But now I'm standing here anyway, at the bar in this 2006 version of a Wild East saloon, drinking beer and chatting with some pretty boy with uncut, pop-star tousled hair and white, even teeth. He must be new here in town, I've never seen him before.
    "Where are you from?"
    "I'm from Great Britain, but my mother is Italian and my father is French."
    "But you're a Brit? Did you grow up in London?"
    "Mostly in Addis Abeba, until I started studying at Oxford."
    "And how did you end up here?"
    "I work for a Spanish aid organization."
    I make an encouraging noise, and he continues. Standard

phrases about himself and his job, as if pulled from a well-written application letter.

"And you? Where are you from?"

My mother is Swedish, my father is Swedish, I grew up in Sweden and work for Sweden. I have only one native language and that's Swedish.

"Will you excuse me for a minute?"

I smile and nod vaguely in some direction. And then I disappear toward the exit. I have to get some air.

I can't stand those people. And I also envy them. The ones who have always moved around the world as a matter of course. My childhood's trips consisted of driving around Uppland in an overloaded blue Ford Escort with my family – a mother, three children, two dogs, a cat. One of my first memories is of my mother telling me to watch out for used syringes in the flowerbed outside the highrise apartment in Gottsunda where we once lived. The only brush with the bigger world outside that we had there was passing some Finnish immigrants in the stairwell. How I wish I could trade what little I have of suburban street cred (nothing at all to brag about in Afghanistan) – for their confidence. How I would love to be able to remember some happy summer vacations on the Riviera!

The evening is mild and the stars are out. You can see the stars so clearly here; there's no interference from city lights, since the city isn't illuminated. There are only some scattered lamps here and there, by a door or a wall, or in some intersection. Otherwise the city is in darkness, tonight like every other night. The sky looks different than it does back home; the constellations are different on this side of the globe, and the strong light makes the sky feel closer. Both heaven and hell are closer to us over here.

At the gate leading out to the street, a few guards sit at their post, with caps and shiny boots, and the obligatory weapons, Kalashnikovs – always Kalashnikovs. How many of them are there in the world? Way too many. One heritage of the war is cheap Kalashnikovs, writes Paul Collier in The Bottom Billion, a book about the mind-boggling billion people who find themselves at the very bottom of the world. The men give me an alert look as they sit there slumped on their chairs; they nod, mumble goodbye.

Wahab is lying asleep in the front seat when I knock on the armored body of the car. He looks happy to be able to go home already. We drive through the empty streets in silence. What exactly is going on in there behind the walls? Will we ever be able to get any insight into the everyday life of Afghan people, other than when some bomb lands in the wrong place, or when some American special forces storm a house in a hunt for a suspected terrorist? Will I, or young Mr. Polyglot in the bar, with his fine set of teeth, ever contribute anything to this place, other than good intentions? Suddenly it feels as if everything that seemed so understandable before is gone. The confidence that what we're doing is, if not always completely right, at least a little bit meaningful – gone.

Parties are a Workday Routine
[February 2006]

Farah Province is one of the lesser known spots on the Afghan map. During the whole time that I've been in the country, I've barely heard a word about what's happening there. There's no one there to report back. So we go there – Tomas, Martine, Amir, and I – to do some fact finding.

It's the beginning of February, 2006, when we leave Kabul. I'm not feeling very well – I have an earache – but the last thing I want to do is miss this trip.

"Are you really sure you should go if you're getting sick?" asks Agneta, the administrator sent by Sida, a woman with a heart of gold.

"Oh, I've had ear infections a hundred times before."

Agneta looks doubtfully at me.

"I can't just hang around here in Kabul all the time. 'A desk is a dangerous place from which to watch the world', as they say."

It's quite possible that it's even more dangerous to watch it from the Farah Province, but I don't feel like testing my worn out maxim just now. I grab a package of antibiotic with an expired "best before"-date from the box of medicines, bandages, and morphine syringes in the office, and off we go.

We're staying at the home of the province's only foreign aid worker, a German engineer who barely knows a word of Dari or Pashto – or English for that matter. He is one of the anonymous heroes of the aid movement. How he survives there completely alone, or what made him settle down in that particular spot, I'm never able to find out, either because my German is too sketchy, or because there's no good answer. But on behalf of his organization, based somewhere in prosperous Germany, he's building schools and digging ditches in this remote spot that remains unreached by any other aid, this poor and dangerous Taliban stronghold.

We visit the governor, Ezatullah Wasefi, at his residence, a modest house with browned grass surrounded by a high cement wall. His saddled horse stands tethered to a pole. He invites us to lunch, served up under a canopy that's been erected over the bottom of his empty swimming pool outside the house.

The talkative governor removes the jacket of his brown suit and hangs it on a plastic chair, revealing the pistol he wears in a leather holster, and sits down. He apologizes for only being able to offer us soda as he hands the cans around the table.

Wasefi episomizes Karzai's appointment policy. He is the son of an influential and esteemed man. That is his main qualification. Other highlights of his resume include a stint in jail for drug-related crimes in the USA, where he lived for many years, and jobs in the restaurant business. What did it say again in the Afghanistan Compact, the agreement that was made between the country's government and all the donor countries when new billions in aid money were about to be promised?

"[The Afghan Government] will recruit competent and credible professionals to public service on the basis of merit; establish a more effective, accountable and transparent administration at all levels of Government; and implement measurable improvements in fighting corruption, upholding justice and the rule of law and promoting respect for the human rights of all Afghans."[4]

Merit-based appointments were promised in order to ensure a more effective use of authority. With that goal in mind, a convicted drug criminal with a pistol tucked into the lining of his pants, and with experience managing pizzas, must be the right man for the job, a worthy representative of the government in one of the country's 34 provinces. Or maybe the president harbors the optimistic hope that this English-speaking governor will work well with the aid community? Or that his cowboy style will work with George W. Bush? That could be one explanation,

---

4   North Atlantic Treaty Organization, *The Afghanistan Compact*, 2006, www.nato.int/isaf/docu/epub/pdf/afghanistan_compact.pdf, p. 4

if it weren't for the fact that there really aren't any westerners in the area for Wasafi to impress. And that President Bush isn't headed to the area either. Nor would I bet my retirement money on the likelihood that a man dressed in Western clothes, who brags about his alcohol consumption like a teenager, will be popular with the Taliban sympathizers in the area. Sometimes I'm tempted to think that I've landed in some sitcom version of the Truman Show. It can't really be true.

But it is true. We want so much and we try everything we can. There just aren't any guarantees.

We eat rice and shishkebab and talk about the situation in the province. We are careful to ask about where we can go. You can go to that village, but you have to avoid that road. You can go to the west, but not to the north, not to Bala Boluk where the Taliban still rule. You can go there but not there. You can meet this person but not that one. We dutifully note the names of places and suitable people to talk to. I feel tired, but elated. Reality nearly always outdoes fiction; I only have to look around me as I sit there on the bottom of the swimming pool, drinking Pepsi. At moments like this there's nothing I'd rather be doing, nowhere else I'd rather be. At moments like this I could die for my job, the best job in the world.

"Are you OK, Princess?" asks Amir surreptitiously in the car on the way back to the guesthouse a few hours later, after the day's meetings.
  If he weren't Afghan I would think he's flirting with me.
  "Just a little tired."
  I force a smile. I don't feel very princess-like now, more as if I've been marinated in dust. And I'm so unbelievably tired. I've also lost my hearing in one ear. I can barely hear anything anymore.

Evening in Farah. Amir is lying on the couch in the TV room, watching BBC World and repeating everything that's said, out loud. That's how he's learned his perfect British English, almost entirely on his own. No English lessons, no textbooks. Still I hear him use words I myself never say. Martine and Tomas are eating dinner with our host the engineer. I'm too tired to eat. Listlessly I fidget with my box of penicillin. I have to do something.

Sitting down in the garden with my satellite phone, I dial the on-call service at the MFA, and ask to be connected to the doctor there. After a moment I have her on the line. The sky is crystal clear, I'm sitting on a cold cement bridge under a roof of dried grapevines and I hear my voice bouncing across the globe. I explain who I am and where I am, tell her about my earache, and that I've lost my hearing.

"You need to see a doctor," she says decisively. "Immediately."

"But I don't think you understand. I'm in western Afghanistan, in the middle of nowhere. This is the middle of nowhere, even by local standards," I explain. "And I don't know if you've ever been in an Afghan hospital, but I have. I'm not going there, not voluntarily."

The image of some dirty, bloodstained floors in a hospital in Kunduz appears with unexpected clarity before my eyes. The dirty coats of the doctors, rows of dirty patients sitting hunched over on beds without sheets, a dank smell of dirt, hopelessness, and death.

"You only have one hearing, two ears. It could be something serious," she insists.

"I'm not even sure there is any doctor or any hospital here," I defend myself.

What wouldn't I give for the much maligned Swedish health clinics right now! If only I had a queue to line up in, I would happily line up. What wouldn't I give to spend five hours in a bare waiting room with coffee from a vending machine and worn out back issues of Swedish women's magazines.

"Then you'll have to go and find a doctor somewhere else," she says sternly.

I don't have the energy to explain any more. For example, that the next flight out from here – the one with five seats – is only leaving in a few days' time, and I'm already booked on it. But we agree that I'll start the course of antibiotics. I promise to try to get to a doctor, mostly so that she won't be angry with me. Then

I fall into a deep sleep, like someone knocked out by Ivan Drago in Rocky IV.

It's the next day. I don't know how I got out of bed. We drive along almost nonexistent roads between the villages that are less dangerous, according to our experts; areas where the Taliban have less influence. As the day goes by I grow steadily more tired and more sluggish. Amir, who's interpreting for me, whispers in the ear that I can technically still hear with, but I have a hard time concentrating, and I'm tired beyond belief.
"Princess, how are you feeling?" asks Amir.
I smile wanly.
"I think I have to go back to the house," I whisper.
Once we get there I crash.

The next morning, I go to the American PRT (Provincial Reconstruction Team) that's located just outside the city of Farah. It's one of the smaller ones, a hundred men, a woman or two. With only a hundred people, any activity in enemy country outside the barbed wire is out of the question. They have to focus on keeping themselves safe in their camp, and even that is a challenge.

The car has to drop me off 150 meters from the gate, since it's forbidden to drive closer than that. I go through the first checkpoint, which is guarded by Afghans; they let me pass without question. When I get at the entrance, a few American soldiers are standing there in full combat gear – the night before, they were attacked with some grenades, and now they're in a state of highest preparedness. I don't have time to introduce myself.
"Ma'am, this is a combat zone! What are you doing here?"
Thank you so much for asking. Well, where should I begin? How many hours do you have? This is my job. I don't know why I became a diplomat. A dream about making a difference. I wanted to travel, learn foreign languages, escape the country. Maybe that's why. Now I guess I'm still here because I don't really know how to do anything else. I travel, speak foreign languages, and for the most part I like living in exile. And sometimes I make a difference.

"I am a diplomat, just visiting. I got sick. I thought you must have a doctor, a proper one."

"Are you American?"

"Swedish."

The soldier looks at my tired appearance, in jeans and a sweatshirt with a scarf sloppily wound around my head, and grabs his radio. A few minutes later a friendly soul comes to meet me and leads me to the medical station.

The doctor is chewing gum and asks me a thousand questions. He can't see any visible inflammation in the ear and thinks the inflammation must be in the middle ear.

"I'll give you this penicillin instead. It works more broadly than the one you started taking. It should work."

He gives me a friendly smile and hands over the little bag of pills.

You have to expect a little collateral damage to get rid of a bad thing.

I go back to the bare, empty house and sleep.

Tomas, Martine, and Amir come and fetch me after their meetings and we finish up the day by going to have dinner with the PRT commander. I'm so tired, so absolutely exhausted, but I wobble along.

In the dining room, a fantastic American dinner awaits us, with tons of fattening food and vegetables I haven't seen in months, and ice cream and muffins and artificially colored sodas. Every gram is imported, even the water has been flown here from the United Arab Emirates. That way the soldiers get the food they're used to, and the food is kept free of parasites. That way, also, the local economy has no opportunity to get a boost from the international presence.

The leader is pleasant and enthusiastic. He has a pitchfork sewn into his uniform jacket and he sees possibilities everywhere. He paints castles in the air in pretty pastel colors about how well everything is going, and in response to our concrete questions, he slithers as skillfully as the serpent in the garden of Eden. He seems to see Afghanistan through two drinking straws, and whatever he sees through them, he presents in a friendly and well-spoken manner.

We have gotten as far as coffee and a scrumptious brownie wrapped in plastic when I notice that I'm drooling. It isn't because of the dessert. It's just that I can't really control myself. I excuse myself and wander off to the medical center. The same nice doctor again.

"I don't know what happened," I slur.

He takes blood samples, asks me to walk along a straight line on the floor.

"Well, you haven't had a stroke."

I laugh, but my face doesn't want to obey me so I fall silent. This isn't funny at all. He keeps tapping at my reflex points, asks me to make a face, stares right in my face. I feel a bad feeling growing inside me.

"I'm not quite sure, but it seems that you have a partial facial paralysis."

For the first time in a year and a half in Afghanistan, I'm terrified. Parasites, stomach aches, cold – sure. Suicide bombers, kidnappings, rockets – sure. But this?

"Hard to say what's triggered it, it might be your inner ear inflammation. Or a long period of stress, or exhaustion. Or something else."

"Do you have a photo of yourself? An ID card or passport, or something? Or do you normally look like this?"

He hands me a mirror with a plastic handle.

I take the mirror with shaking hands. Yes, that's me. I still recognize myself. It's only when I smile that one side of my face doesn't want to cooperate; it prefers to stay sulky.

"In most cases by far, this resolves itself within six to eight weeks," he says, packaging pills in different bags.

It's a good thing that I'm sitting on the examining table, I'm not sure my legs would hold me. I follow his every movement.

"If it is what I think it is, that is."

I don't say anything.

"Take three a day of these, and two per day of these, four of these. And also continue with the penicillin. And then two weeks of sick leave. Minimum."

Life as a diplomat, where parties are part of the workday routine.

When the only plane of the week arrives a few days later, Amir, Martine, and Tomas fly on to the Nimruz Province, while I fly home with my little bags of pills and my anxiety, and go on sick leave.

What do you do in Kabul without work? It's dead boring. Uneventful. All I want to do is fast forward myself two months to see if I'll look normal again, if the lopsidedness will fix itself. But no. The days have never passed as slowly, time seems to move backwards. I sleep, read, watch movies, and sleep some more. I write in order to tamp down my anxiety. I walk around in my house and turn the knobs of the radiators. I drink tea. I try to come up with a few new recipes based on the same old ingredients. I look at myself in the mirror twenty times a day and look for changes, signs that I'm getting better. Signs of normality. After a week, I'm back at the office again.

No One Could Be Safer
[February 2006]

A day off. Wrapped in scarves and sweaters, I'm walking around at home, puttering. I call my mother, thinking that she'll want to hear that her daughter is alive. A sign of life.

"Hi, Mom!"

A little static electricity hitchhikes between the continents, then my mother's familiar voice.

"Hi, sweetheart. How are things? Where are you?"

"Everything's fine. I'm at home."

"Oh, how nice! Are you in Stockholm!!"

"No, at home in Kabul. In my house."

"Oh, I see. Yes. Everything's fine here too. And the crocuses have come up! Just think! Already! I was out in the garden early this morning and then I had my morning coffee on the veranda, and the sun was really warm."

"How wonderful that sounds! Over here..."

"It's so nice that the days are starting to get lighter."

I look for some piece of furniture to sit down on. I really wish I hadn't called.

"Really. The power is gone completely here, I'm cold most of the..."

"And my medicine came in the mail last week."

"Medicine? Did something happen? Are you sick?"

I hear my voice going up a notch.

"No, no, you don't need to worry about me! I got some Tamiflu. I didn't want to take any risks! You don't have to worry about me, sweetheart!"

But I wish someone would worry about me a little. Just a little bit. Just enough.

"No, of course not, not at all."

I summon new strength.

"But Tamiflu? I didn't know the bird flu had come to Sweden. Isn't it just in Asia that it's a problem?" I say.

I mean, "here in Asia".

"No, it's here too. Last week a case was reported in Germany. In the Baltic!"

I can't hide my surprise.

"Yes, but that's pretty far away..."

Of course – newspapers and TV in the safety-addicts' paradise have reported on some stray dead swan in the Baltic Sea. Banal and dumbed down at best, mocking and making everything ridiculous at worst. Sometimes Sweden seems to me to be oriented away from the urgent things. It's so much easier that way. Why care about the thousands of people who are dying every day from malnutrition, childbirth, dirty water, malaria? As long as it isn't Europeans who are dying, or Americans, it's as if they don't count.

"I just can't take any risks," my mother continues, triggered by my silence. "It'll be here anytime. But now I have Tamiflu, so don't you worry."

"That's good..."

We hang up. I stay sitting on the stool with my cell phone in my hand. I've never felt further away from my family, from everyone who should be close to me. A strange bird.

Temptations [March 2006]

One evening when I go to work out, I take a bottle of fine whisky with me for Matti as a thank you for being my punching bag. He calls up me an hour or two later.

"Was that whisky thing a joke, or what?" he says with his dragging Finnish accent.

"What? No, what do you mean?"

"I can even see the tea leaves in it."

I hang up, run to my liquor cabinet and inspect the bottles. The gin is water, the vodka too. And didn't I have a lot of wine bottles? And what happened to that carton of vodka I had with me when I moved? Everything's gone. And then there was the time when I came home and the whole house smelled bad, and I found Malalai sleeping on the floor on my clean laundry, with vomit next to her on the wall to wall carpet. Maybe she didn't have the stomach flu after all?

When Malalai comes, I cross examine her. "Why?" I ask. "What else?" I ask. She denies, I persist. She just shakes her head, looking down stubbornly at the table.

"I want my keys back, and you are not welcome back here," I finally say.

"But I have such low wages!" she sniffs.

"So you admit it!"

"I won't do it again. I promise!"

"Malalai, I can't have someone I don't trust coming and going in my house, someone who steals my things. It won't work."

"But how will I provide for my children?" she sobs. "Now I'll have to go out on the street!"

For several days afterwards, she comes to my office and cries. But it doesn't work. My heart has grown hard as titanium, and it's covered in ice.

An Afghan Star [March 2006]

One of my rare consular cases reaches me. A cry for help from an organization that works with freedom of the press and endangered journalists finds its way to my office. They're wondering if there's anything Sweden can do for an Afghan journalist, Shakeb Isaar, who has been receiving death threats.

Shakeb is a program director. Together with a female colleague, he plays music videos in one of Tolo TV's most popular programs, *Hop.* Tolo TV is the country's only private channel, owned by two Afghan brothers who spent most of their lives in Australia but have now returned to Afghanistan. Every day they stretch the boundaries of what is accepted and allowed. They broadcast Turkish and Indian pop videos. They have programs with health tips and home exercise for the country's women who can't leave their homes. They have their own version of extreme makeover, where young Afghans with shalwar kamiz and beards are spiffed up with Western clothes and a clean shave. They have female program directors – some of whom even appear on the screen along with their male colleagues. This must be the "change from within" that Baqer Moin was talking about. Tolo TV is a peaceful revolution, a daily rebellion on screen.

Not everyone shares my delight in Tolo TV. The mullahs grumble, and others too – they complain that the channel threatens the Afghan culture and Islam. And in May 2005, one of many threats was carried out – Shakeb's coworker in the program, the female program director Shaima Rezayee, was shot to death.

I meet Shakeb Isaar in a little conference room at Tolo TV's office, where he's been hiding. He is cute as anything with his pop hairstyle, his jeans, and his hip clothes; he could easily be a model for a JC clothing ad. But he hangs his head, and his eyes look dead.
"I do not even dare to go home," he says.
After Shaima's death, he is no longer able to brush off the threats.

"I can't promise anything," I say. "It's hard."

I send the request to the Swedish Migration Board representative at the embassy in Islamabad and ask if there's anything at all we can do.

A few days later, I get the answer that we can arrange a visa for Shakeb. Once he's in Sweden, he'll be able to seek asylum. Then it's for the Migration Board to decide if his application will be approved. It can take months to sort out. Wahab drives me to Tolo TV's office.

On the days when I wonder what I'm doing, and if I can even make any difference at all, I will think of this day.

Shakeb doesn't dare believe it's true; he's happy as a child. I put on the brakes, do what I can to take down his expectations a notch. So much can still go wrong. I say that nothing is resolved, he may not receive asylum in the end, you never know. But there's some breathing room, maybe the dust will settle here in the meantime. I try to explain that it won't be easy over there. I struggle to express what I mean. Here he has everything: a context, a job, a family. Close to movie star status. There, he'll arrive empty-handed. Here he is everything, there he will be...no one. Just one more anonymous asylum seeker in some refugee center with orange curtains, broken shutters, mismatched furniture, and shabby bed linens. He's a journalist, completely dependent on his language; over there he won't be able to get work as a journalist unless his Swedish is perfect. It's so hard to explain. He smiles with his whole body, and all I can do is paint life in Sweden in the blackest black.

He looks at me without understanding.

"But Diana, I cannot stay here. I just want to live."

We sit there in silence for a moment.

It's hard to argue with that.

A week or two go by. The organization rustles up the money for his plane ticket and some pocket money. He's afraid that he'll be stopped at Kabul's airport. I'm more worried that they'll send him back once he gets to Frankfurt, in spite of his Swedish Schengen visa. He wonders how everything will turn out – he's never been to Europe before. Like so many other Afghans, his life has played out entirely around Afghanistan and its borders – in Pakistan, Uzbekistan, and Turkmenistan.

His visa papers come back from the embassy in Islamabad, and I drive them over to him. Yet again I explain what he needs to do when he arrives at Arlanda airport, go through what he can expect in the coming months, emphasize that he may not be able to stay there at all in the end, and warn that it will be hard. A few more days go by, and he's on his way.

He calls me from Frankfurt, wondering where to go.
"Go to Stockholm, and there you'll just do exactly what I told you."

From Arlanda airport he calls again, in the middle of the night.
"What do I do now?"
I see him before me, alone at Arlanda. Everyone else has disappeared; they all have somewhere to go. And there he stands with his whole life in a suitcase, completely alone in the world.
"Get hold of the first official you see and tell them you've come to seek asylum," I explain, for what must be the tenth time.
"They know you're coming at the Migration Board, they're expecting you. They'll take care of the rest."
I hang up, toss and turn in bed a little longer, wonder how it's going, wonder how he is, wonder whether his joy at being able to start over somewhere else has been replaced by a gnawing feeling of doubt. And of course, his exile is not voluntary like mine.

He ends up at a refugee center in Ludvika, a small town in central Sweden. I so wish that he won't experience what I've experienced in Kabul. Living in a parallel world, aside from my contacts with officials. The only acquaintance I have from Ludvika is Anders, alias the pop singer Moneybrother. I give him a call.
"Do you know anyone who can take him on? Take him out to eat somewhere? Give him a way in to Swedish society? I don't

want him to sit there by himself, half the globe away from his context."

Anders thinks it over.

"I'll check with a girl I know who's still in Ludvika."

But when I talk to Shakeb, he's feeling optimistic, not nearly as worried as I am. We talk about this and that, I remind him that he has to study Swedish until his eyes cross. He tells me about what he's doing, articles that were written about him, jobs he wants to apply for. He hangs out with the other people there – Iraqis, Kurds, Somalis – and plays soccer. He's started taking Swedish lessons. He reads.

"Diana, thank you so much for everything. I am so happy."

"Don't thank me. I was just doing my job."

"I realize now that we live like dogs in Afghanistan. Like dogs."

Swedish Authorities [March 2006]

The courier post arrives. Among all these letters from my bank – my most faithful pen pal these days – there's an envelope with a plastic window, from the Audio and Braille Library, a place I've never heard of before. A neat A4-size letter informs me that the small 32-page publication that I wrote for the Institute of International Affairs has now been recorded as an audiobook. In case the audiobook is checked out from a library, I will be compensated at the rate of a few cents per loan.

I tape the letter to my refrigerator door as a reminder that there are other, parallel worlds.

Spring Sun [March 2006]

Not too far from the Titanic Market – the place where during Taliban times there was a black market that sold pirated cassettes and DVDs of *Titanic* – is the Taliban photographer. At least, that's the name I've given him after hearing about the photographs he takes with a box camera, and then colors by hand, like in a bygone era. Is he being ironic? Political? Or has he just carved out a niche in the market that no one else filled? I have no idea, but I want to have some Taliban photos.

Said and done. A few weeks later, I head over there along with Clinton, a young American who in no time at all has learned the language and everything that's worth knowing in town. Clinton is cute, charming, and smart, and looks like he is 19 years old. I wish I could fall for him; he's so completely decent. We could live in an American small town with two cars in the driveway, be members of the Rotary Club, and have apple-cheeked kids who eat Frosted Flakes for breakfast. But it's no use, however much he makes me laugh.

It's a lukewarm day in March, a day when all the gray is gone. The houses and the walls are tinged with more of a golden yellow color – just look! I've seen it wrong all winter, it isn't gray at all. The mountains surrounding the city stretch proudly toward the blue sky. Everywhere I see tiny little signs, glimpses of another Afghanistan, a country that's hungry for the future. The kiosks that crowd each other in the city center, where you can buy Bollywood movies, CDs with Turkish pop, or cell phones, pots, and synthetic rope; the road workers who are repairing holes in the road; a donkey that looks well-groomed and well-fed as it trods past energetically with its load tied to a wooden cart; some young women in jeans and scarves, leaning against a wall, laughing until their bodies shake. The produce stands with pyramids of well-polished vegetables.

The photographer has a little studio squeezed in among the kiosks on the west bank of the Kabul River. Which isn't always a river – for eleven months out of the year it's just clay and trash. But today, I don't see that.

He arranges the styling with solemn care. We're posed as if for a wedding photo, against a garish backdrop of a colorful mountain landscape. Clinton is given a turban, camouflage jacket, and Kalashnikov made of plastic to pose with; I'm given a burka, from which I peer out (in the background, of course), and a bouquet of plastic flowers, colorful like a disco ball.

"No, don't smile! Chin down!"

Then he ducks under the cloth.

How can I help smiling? It's so liberating to sit in central Kabul with someone whose business idea is mocking the Taliban era and its ideals.

Afterwards I go to Serena, the city's newly opened and fanciest hotel. I sit in its little kelim-decorated café, my new favorite place since the hotel opened, and drink tea. Today it pains me that the countdown to my departure has begun. In spite of pressure from the MFA, I've decided not to extend my contract a second time. I was tired and grumpy when they called. And now I'm sitting here with all this on one side of the balance – my life here, my friends, my city, my job – and nothing but uncertainty on the other.

Farewell to Arms [April 2006]

The village mosque is full when we arrive. It's as hot as a kiln inside. Men are sitting in rows on the floor. They've come from the surrounding villages, on foot or by donkey. One man has a hunting rifle with him. Around his upper body he wears a leather ammunition belt, filled with shotgun shells. He reminds me of a 1910 version of a wild-eyed Rambo. A few others have their Kalashnikovs securely within arm's reach.

Michael, an Irishman with alert blue eyes and as much energy as a nuclear power plant, has asked me to come along to witness the disarming of illegal militias. Commander Didar wants to show that he's a good candidate before the upcoming parliamentary election by trying to convince his home village to disarm.

"I've promised to bring some foreign witnesses with me," Michael explains, rolling his eyes.

No sooner said than done. We are six witnesses from the world community itself, bumping along the through the streets of Kabul, empty on a Friday, headed toward Khak Jabar. The sun is shining, the weather gods are out of step with pallid everyday Afghanistan. Commander Didar and his bodyguards skid along the gravel ahead of us in a Land Cruiser and a pickup truck. A recently built building with reflective glass windows rises up among the ruins. We follow the dried-out flood bed out of the city.

After a little more than an hour we approach Khak Jabar. If nothing else, you can tell by the fact that Commander Didar's election poster is plastered onto almost every rock and every wall: a man with uncompromising features, a bushy pirate beard, and *pakul*. With posters, weapons, threats, and pressure, he hopes to win a place in parliament and secure his political future in the election some months away. Shortly thereafter, we reach Khord Kabul, the commander's home village. It's a collection of mud houses exposed to the unforgiving, scorching rays of the sun.

We squeeze into the crowded mosque. There is no women's section, and women are generally not welcome at the Friday prayer, but my two colleagues and I are taken to the side room, followed by curious smiles. We don't fit into any Afghan rule system in any case. If Michael's bushy beard weren't red, he could easily pass for an Afghan today, with his green turban and his light blue shalwar kamiz. Commander Didar, who hasn't been to the village in more than three years, summons up his courage, stands, and gives his fiery speech. He has an arrogant smile that rarely leaves his lips but never reaches his eyes. He talks about ethnic unity, about good relationships with Iran and Pakistan, and about the village's troubles. He talks about the blood feud with the Akmedzai tribe that he wants to put behind him. He throws in a line about women's situation, certainly not completely uinfluenced by the three pairs of eyes that are watching him from the side room. And finally he says: "Disarm! Weapons only cause trouble! Once I have been elected to parliament, I will take care of your problems in Kabul!"

Commander Didar sits down and wipes the sweat from his forehead. Murmuring breaks out. Maybe they are opposed. Maybe they're pointing out that all trust was used up long ago in this country. Maybe they don't want to give way to his threats, lightly disguised as advice.

A few other people give their input. More murmuring follows. There's prayer. Everyone gets up to leave. *Insh'allah* – Allah willing – a few weapons will be collected, we are told.

The DIAG, or Disarmament of Illegally Armed Groups, is a continuation of the disarming process, in theory already completed, in which Afghan militias were dissolved and replaced with the new, national Afghan army. With DIAG, the hope is to also disarm the estimated 130,000 armed men who are connected to different individuals and illegal militias, beyond the control of the government. Wicked tongues call the project the world's biggest junk collection – what the warlords and others give up, if anything, is unusable junk.

Everyone leaves the mosque, and we come out onto the street. Rows of plates with scented pilaf and kebab and steaming rice are laid out on the ground. Our group is divided up, and we women are shown to a room with women lined up all along the walls. We sit down on some pillows. The feeling that life is playing out somewhere else has rarely been so palpable. The conversation is halting.

"Pashto?" someone asks.

I shake my head.

"Urdu?"

No, not that either.

In this group of women clad in head scarves, there's one woman who knows some Dari. She's thirty years old and has nine children. One of the children, about two years old, is clinging to her lap and wants to nurse.

"How many children do you have?" she asks with a smile, exposing her almost toothless gums.

I've heard that it's the many years of nursing that make the women lose their teeth so early.

"None," I answer.

She looks at me in shock.

All the women along the walls stare at me with horror.

"And you?" she asks, nodding toward my colleagues.

They shake their heads.

The conversation comes to a dead stop. Our hostesses look down at the rug. How silly and vain it is to imagine that they see any kind of role models in us westerners as we travel around the country, or that we could make them see that another reality is possible. When they look at us, they don't see women with careers, opinions of their own, money, and freedom to do what they want. They see some lost souls who haven't covered their hair properly and who have been punished with childlessness by Allah.

The silence has become so dense and oppressive that we decide to thank the women and take our leave. Before we go, we each receive a scarf as a gift. Mine is lavender and made of polyester.

We join the rest of our group for lunch. It's the same food as always: pilaf, chicken, kebab, spinach cooked to a mush, and freshly baked bread. And Pepsi and Fanta in cans – wherever I go there are cans of Pepsi and Fanta, at every single meal to which I've been invited, in every little village. Rarely or never penicillin and midwives, but always canned soda.

I dig in to the kebab – it is now months since I gave up trying to be a vegetarian. For two decades, I've motivated my reluctance to eat meat with the fact that I don't like how slaughterhouses are run. And I really don't like it. But here I only feel silly with my Western ideas. Slaughterhouses? Here? And to be too finicky to eat the food that's offered in a country where half the population goes to bed hungry, that simply doesn't work. That goes against my grain even more.

I eat rice from the same plate as Commander Didar, but try to keep to an uncontaminated side of the plate, just in case his bloodthirstiness and barbarism are contagious.

"Will any weapons be collected?" Michael demands.

Commander Didar squirms uncomfortably.

"Insh'allah."

He wipes some beads of sweat from his brow with his scarf and continues.

"The villagers feel that it's difficult. They can't come forward with weapons now, since they've said before that they didn't have any."

"Of course," Michael laughs and rolls his eyes.

"Anyway, maybe there aren't any weapons," Didar adds defensively.

No, indeed. If there are no weapons here, then it must be the only spot in all of Afghanistan that has no weapons.

But I've already understood that Commander Didar doesn't intend to contribute to the disarmament efforts. It's always someone else who has to do something. The other villagers, the other warlords, the United Nations, the United States, Pakistan, Iran – anyone at all, as long as it's someone else. The idea of personal responsibility has never quite taken root in Afghan society, built as it is on collective thinking.

After lunch, we go and look at some emptied weapon depots. There are a few empty holes in the ground.

"Well?" Michael wonders.

"Ah, hm..."

Commander Didar gropes for excuses, scratching his beard.

Maybe there won't be any weapon collection after all. You never know. Insh'allah it will work, we're told.

We visit a clinic just outside the village. The little building has recently been constructed by German military, but is completely empty. There is no doctor here, they complain.

"No one at all?"

We are upset that clinics are built but can't be staffed by anyone. This is discussed for a while, from various angles. And then it turns out that there is a doctor, after all – one. But he is in Pakistan on vacation now.

"One doctor, is that all?"

A new discussion breaks out. No, actually, there's a nurse too, who sees patients for a few hours every day except on Fridays.

We don't stay to hear if there's any physical therapy, surgery room, maternal healthcare or long-term care. I don't think there is, but who knows? Here nothing is what it seems to be. Expect the unexpected, as my German colleague used to say, summing up two decades of experience in the country.

Instead we return to the village to see how the weapon collection is going. There are still no weapons in sight. Commander Didar is – or pretends to be – worried.

"But how will anyone be able to turn in their weapons when they've claimed for so long that they don't have any?" he repeats.

Michael laughs at this weak excuse.

"You must know that Afghanistan has two export products," he tells me.

"First of all, the country supplies 87 percent of the world's heroin. Secondly, it supplies nearly 90 percent of the world's excuses."

We have completely given up hope that any weapons will be collected today. Instead, we enjoy the sunshine and the mountains, and being far away from the dust of Kabul.

But Commander Didar doesn't want to look like he is unable to deliver. He takes us to a building just outside the town. Near the wall there's a little pile of rusting ammunition from World War I. Didar looks infinitely satisfied. His bodyguards are helping to carry out some rifles from an outhouse. They are rusty and covered in clay and dust, with a patina of spiderwebs. The only way they could cause any harm is if they're used to hit someone with, or if you trip over them. As the crowning glory, these rifles are laid on top of the pile of ammunition. I examine the pathetic little pile. It's a telling example of the Afghan disarmament process.

"That's all there is," says Commander Didar.

He brushes off a little clay and dust from his hands.

"Insh'allah."

Hope [April 2006]

I've found Oasis, a beauty parlor in Qal-e Fatullah. I go there sometimes and practice my halting Farsi with the giggling girls, as they serve tea and try to touch up my increasingly shabby facade. These pockets of another Afghanistan are what give me hope and make me feel so happy. They can keep me smiling for a long time, until the nail polish begins to chip many, many days later.

Ministry of Refugees [April 2006]

I'm sitting in an unlit corridor at the Ministry of Refugees and Repatriations, waiting to make yet another attempt to get a readmission agreement between Sweden and Afghanistan in place, when the phone rings.

"Hi, it's Martin."

That voice, so familiar and yet so strange.

"Hi there."

Am I able to hide my surprise? Hardly. He knows me too well. It's been months since we've been in touch, in any case months since he's been in touch.

"I'm standing outside the Afghan embassy in Paris. I need an invitation for my visa."

"Your visa?"

"Yes, the old one expired. Last chance to come, right?"

"Well, yes. What are you doing in Paris?"

"Vacation."

"I see," I say, although I don't see at all.

Martin, who didn't want to leave our neighborhood when I wanted to do something, see something, travel. Now, suddenly, he's vacationing in Paris. I should be happy, but my first instinct is just to feel jealous, of whomever or whatever it is that's suddenly making him visit Paris. It's no consolation that I'm the one he's calling now and wants to visit.

"I'll fax an invitation to the embassy, no problem. I'll be back at the office in an hour or two."

The stream of ones and zeros through the ether are interrupted, and I'm back in the unlit corridor. It's long after the scheduled appointment, but the man I'm supposed to meet isn't there. Maybe he's forgotten that I'm coming. I'm given tea, and men and women smile and apologize as they rush past the armchair where I've been stranded. Martin. I wonder what he wants and what he intends to do, if anything.

Back at the office I fax a new invitation. He gets a new visa. He doesn't come this time either. The difference is enormous – this time I discover it doesn't make any difference whatsoever to me.

Kill Them [Spring 2006]

I'm sitting at the Flower Café, enjoying some pale rays of spring sun, when I happen to talk to Malalai, an educated attorney raised in New York. She's thin, well-dressed, and so cool that the temperature in the garden where I'm sitting sinks a few degrees when she makes her entrance. Malalai works as advisor at the Ministry of Water and Energy, where the conservative warlord Ismail Khan is the current minister. Her husband works as an advisor to President Karzai. I don't know either of them very well, but I've heard about their ultra conservative Pashtun wedding in New York. I can see it before me: the men in one group, the women in another – heavily made up, dressed to the teeth – hours of bellowing music through raspy speakers, tables laden with cans of Fanta and heaping plates of food. If I think I'm living in parallel worlds, then what is she doing? I can't make the image of those two fit together – Malalai seems to need her husband as much as a fish needs a bicycle. She's social and forward-thinking, while he just seems cunning. We drink pomegranate juice and talk about this and that until the conversation, as it always does here, glides over to the situation in the country, and security.

"Sometimes it feels so hopeless," I sigh. "Where to begin?"

She licks a little juice from her lips and sets down her glass.

"You have to start by killing a lot of people. The warlords, the ones who have ruined the land. They have to be removed."

"Yes, absolutely, they have to be removed, but kill them..." I begin.

To mention the death penalty is like tapping my knee with a rubber mallet. Before I've had time to stop myself, the whole catalog of arguments against it has poured out of me.

"Yes, kill them," Malalaj continues. "If we lock them up, the Afghans will still fear that they'll come out one day. Then they always have to relate to them. They have to disappear, be buried. It's the only way to move forward."

I try to argue that one injustice doesn't justify another. My wet blanket of morals doesn't impress her at all. Morality is not what controls politics, neither here nor elsewhere.

I think about the plan for "transitional justice" – the process of trying those who were guilty of massive human rights violations – that a group of western ambassadors had worked on for months, with great effort, together with the relevant Afghan officials. According to the plan, at least some small steps would be taken to give the victims some kind of restitution, and even if the worst offenders weren't punished, at least they would eventually lose their current positions as police chiefs, ministers, and governors. In the end, when we thought that we had safely landed this brittle project, the president refused to stand behind it on his own. Instead he wanted to present it to the government, where several of the ministers undoubtedly would feel themselves threatened. But he didn't do that either. Instead, nothing at all happened. Foreign pressure weighs little against strong domestic interests. Why wasn't a war crime tribunal set up after the fall of the Taliban? It's hard to see how the country will be able to heal without a national reconciliation process of some kind. Maybe Malalai's ideas are more in step with the political reality, if not with my own ideas about justice; I don't know. What I do think I know after my time here is that it's impossible to turn over a new leaf unless impunity ends and justice is carried out, in one way or another. It won't be possible to put everyone on trial, but everyone can't just be allowed to go free either.

"Shoot them, just shoot them!" says Malalai, pushing the empty glass away from her, as if that decided everything.

Is this adjusted for my ears, or does she say the same thing to Afghans? To her boss?

"But Ismail Khan? How can you work for him? Isn't he one of them, the warlords?"

"He is a very interesting man."

"Yes, but..."

I grope for words to express the obvious arguments, the cracks in her reasoning. Even if Ismail Khan is not considered to be one of the worst warlords, he certainly is no baby dove either. She could hardly be planning to kill him at the ministry in an unguarded moment, could she? Would she shoot him? Pour arsenic in his tea? Several of the returning Afghans seem almost bewitched by the warlords. Is it the proximity to power and influence that attracts and fascinates? The fact that you can go from an everyday grind in the United States to a top job in the Afghan administration "just" because you're Afghan? But Malalai doesn't strike me as someone who was an underdog in the US, flipping burgers at some tired fast food joint. She doesn't seem to be the type that's easily impressed.

The most common argument for why the warlords are still there is that there aren't any other people who are better equipped to do things. At the same time, the international community's exit strategy builds on the notion that someday, at an unknown time, we will be able to leave the country in the Afghans' own hands. But what if they are the same hands that held the controls last time? When the factor that united Afghan's opposition movement – the Soviet occupation – no longer existed, the opposition groups weren't able to unite around a new national leadership. The competition and fragmentation along ethnic lines, language, tribe, religion, and class soon threw the country into a devastating and brutal civil war that plagued it until the Taliban overtook power. In his book *The Bottom Billion*, Paul Collier points to the trap that conflicts make. Low income, slow growth, and a dependence on export of raw materials makes a country prone to conflict: "... [T]he risk that a country in the bottom billion falls into civil war in any five-year period is nearly one in six, the same risk facing a player of Russian roulette." Conflicts give rise to more conflicts. "Civil war leaves a legacy of organized killing that is hard to live down."[5] What indication is there that the same warlords would be able to agree peacefully about how the country should be run this time? Why do they deserve one more chance? Could it really be that among the twenty-five to thirty-five million Afghans, there are none who would be more suitable than this handful of men? I would like to argue that in fact, anyone would be more suitable, that no one could be less suitable than these particular men.

5   Paul Collier, *The Bottom Billion: Why the Poorest Countries Are Failing and What Can Be Done About It.* Oxford University Press, 2007, pp. 32-33.

Admittedly, reforming the national government is an enormous task. To depose a minister or a governor might seem relatively simple, if the protests from the supporting troops are not too loud and violent. The true administrative challenge is handling all the tens of thousands of people who fill the ministries, the governor's administrations, the courts, and so on, who completely lack the necessary competence, and many of whom are corrupt and loyal to some local power player instead of toward Kabul. And with whom could the deposed, incompetent authorities be replaced, in a country where an educated and competent workforce is in such short supply? At the same time, these people do not entail as big a threat to the idea of a better Afghanistan as the warlords who have been reincarnated as police chiefs and ministers. As long as these men still remain, they're a symbol of impunity and a reminder that no one is safe, that history can be repeated.

For every answer I get, there are so many new questions. And before I get any further, something or someone has come between, the conversation has slid over to something else; it's time to hurry on.

Riots, Departure [May/June 2006]

It's May 29 and it starts like a regular day at the office. But then – *expect the unexpected*. In the northern outskirts of Kabul, the brakes fail on a truck that is part of a convoy of the American coalition's vehicles. Twelve cars and several civilians are involved in the crash. As if by magic, a crowd of people has gathered. Shots break out – who shoots at whom first, and why, and how many times? It will never be possible to clarify exactly what happens next. But soon hundreds of people have gathered in Khair Khana in protest and begin marching toward central Kabul. Police checkpoints are set on fire, the police seem to have been swallowed up by the ground, aid offices are attacked, and houses are plundered and vandalized.

The city is simmering with rumors, an improbably boiling pot, an evil witches' brew. My Sida colleagues and I are reached by fragmented and contradictory fragments of information that spread like wildfire. They are impossible to evaluate, but at the same time it's unthinkable not to react to them. In short order the first cellular network stops working, then soon after, the second one.

I gather up official stamps and other things that shouldn't be allowed to fall into the wrong hands, and lock them in the safe in case we have to evacuate. We take down the flags from the building; we've never had any sign on the outside for safety reasons. Time and again I call our security company, but can't get through.

We sit down in the narrow windowless corridor outside my office and wait. We listen to the scattered shooting that's reached even our neighborhood. And the chirping birds; I can't remember ever having heard any before. What kind of birds decide to settle here in Kabul? It must be the depressed ones, the ones with sadistic tendencies, the ascetics. There are almost no trees, no birdbaths, not many breadcrumbs. We drink tea, and eat nuts and dried chickpeas. We talk about everyday things; our mouths move, but our thoughts are somewhere else. What will we do if they come here? We have only one armored car and we can't all fit into it. Should we send the local employees home, or is it safer for them to stay?

I send a short mail to the MFA in Stockholm: *Kabul in convulsions*. Then I hurry back to the corridor. I don't want to sit near any windows, intercept the arc of some stray bullet; I don't want to challenge fate too much. Not in my last days. There isn't that much common sense to brace myself with, so why not some superstition? It almost seems natural.

We sit there like this, for an hour or two, or maybe three. At one point I get through to our security managers.

"I cannot speak right now," the man who answers the phone roars. "We are under attack!"

The conversation is cut off. I carefully place the phone in my lap and bury my face in my hands for a moment.

A few hours later, it's all over. The cell phones start to work again. Some men from our security company come by to check on us. They storm in with automatic weapons and safety vests, their clothes stained with blood; they interrupt each other and talk about how their camp was attacked, vehicles set on fire. It's more a question of how they are than how we are.

"We are fine. Just fine. Luckily it never really reached this part of town."

I force myself to smile a little. "Yes, a little luck never hurts."

I don't have the energy now to think about everything that could have gone wrong. What use is that? You cross a bridge when you reach it. This time – no bridge. Simple.

We all go home. I putter around in my house. It's late afternoon and the silence feels ominous. I make tea. I walk around in my slippers and try to occupy myself, as all the while a bad feeling rises in me like an elevator. Is it really calm? Or is the calm just deceptive? I don't know, I only feel uneasy, the uncertainty of not being able to read the situation, of not even knowing exactly what has happened. For the first time since the first kidnappings occurred when I had just arrived in the country, I feel uneasy being home alone. In Afghanistan, there are no secrets. In spite of the anonymous wall of the house, everyone around knows that a Western woman lives here alone. What if the present calm is deceptive? What do I do if there's a new, angry mob in the neighborhood in a few hours? There are so many groups that might use the anger and frustration, take this opportunity to spread terror among the foreigners. Here a few human lives are worth so little.

I call up a friend – we can call him Sam – a man I got to know many, many years ago. A man with "special skills".

"I don't want to be alone. Not tonight, not after what happened today."

"I should be able to get there in just over an hour," he answers. "I just need to get a few things together."

Then I call Frauke, a friend who is leaving Kabul for good the next morning, after many years in the country. She lives in Shar-e Naw, which borders Qal-e Fatullah, where things were at their worst.

"How are things?"

While I at least have guards at my house and barbed wire along the top of the wall, real locks on the doors and bars on the windows, she has nothing but a latch on her gate.

"I've been sitting under my window all day today with the smell of gunsmoke in my nostrils. Unreal, is how things are," Frauke answers.

"But your *chaukidar* is there, isn't he? You're not completely alone?"

"He disappeared earlier, when the trouble began. He said that his brother had gotten caught in the middle of it and he had to rush to help him."

Ah, what a good excuse to stay away from the foreigners, the natural targets.

"You know, my goodbye party tonight... I guess I should cancel it. But I've made ten liters of spinach soup anyway. I didn't have anything better to do."

We laugh.

"You can sleep here tonight. You shouldn't be alone in your house, not in that neighborhood."

"But what if any of the guests come, and I'm not here?"

"No one's going to leave their house after a day like this, believe me."

She isn't hard to persuade.

I send Wahab to fetch her.

"I go to town?" he says in a falsetto voice.

He makes no effort to hide what a bad idea he thinks it is.

I nod.

"Now?? Tonight???"

Exactly.

With a sigh, he turns the key in the ignition. Kind, wonderful Wahab, someone to depend on in any situation. I'm thinking that it was a long time since I last saw him laugh. He doesn't have a loud or boisterous laugh; it's a smile that spreads over his entire face but above all burrows into his green eyes, without covering up the hint of sadness that's always there. But that was a long time ago. I must ask him how his family is doing, I think. Ask about his daughter who was sick, find out if she received any care in Peshawar.

Frauke comes. My night guards who have arrived now are more alert than I've ever seen them as they carefully bolt the door behind her. Sam comes. He lifts a seventy-liter trunk from the car, slamming the door with so much force that I think it's going to fall off its hinges. My guards look like children on Christmas Eve as their shining eyes move from him, to the trunk he carries in one hand and his automatic weapon in the other.

"Frauke, meet Sam."

They greet each other. She barely reaches up to his armpit. Not many people do.

She looks questioningly at me.

"An old friend."

I make a gesture, an attempt to replace all the answers I don't want to give her.

"Do you want something to drink? I need a drink after this day."

"I'll go take a shower," says Sam. "You know how to handle one of these, don't you?"

He holds up the weapon. I nod silently. But would I really be able to shoot anyone?

"You just have to take aim and shoot. There's a cartridge inside, and the safety latch is here."

He points and then puts down the weapon on the threshold between the kitchen and hallway. Then he disappears upstairs to the bathroom on the second floor.

Frauke and I uncork a bottle of red wine. We make dinner and bake a chocolate cake – a clear symptom of stress. We talk about the insanity, about not knowing what the reaction will be, and about not knowing what has happened. We discuss why you get so superstitious after spending time here, when you're on the threshold of your departure. About why Nato didn't do this or that. About where the Afghan police were, and all the thousands of ISAF soldiers in the city. Again and again, we go through what we saw and heard, and what we didn't see and hear. We sift through and examine the flora of rumors.

"It's going to feel good to leave Afghanistan."

Yes, tonight I can feel it in my whole body. It will feel good to finally be able to relax. I don't feel it so much when I'm here, that alertness that always follows me around the country like a shadow, wherever I go and whatever I do. But as soon as I've landed somewhere else outside the country's borders I notice it, realize that it was left behind somewhere over the Afghan mountains, on the other side of the airplane window.

I think back on the twenty-two months that have passed since I came, and everything that's happened. It's hard to make this country fit into my progressive worldview, I have to admit. More children are attending school, women are allowed to work and enjoy the same rights as the men (at least on paper), mlllions of refugees have been able to return, the country has a president elected by the people, as well as a parliament and a constitution.

This is what I usually point to when I try to defend what we're doing here, what Sweden has achieved at a cost of more than half a billion per year, what the world has achieved for all its billions of dollars and for those who were killed here: soldiers, aid workers, diplomats, and journalists.

But on the other side of the balance there's the ever deteriorating security situation; the president's dubious twilight deals with different groups and phalanxes; the ever more widespread corruption, like a cancer in the body of society; the Taliban's continued gains; the almost complete impunity and the fact that the country's executioners are still allowed to be main actors in the political game; an inferior education system; the bigger and bigger opium harvests; the increasing regional instability, and an oversized but underperforming administration.

And yet, just because it isn't easy doesn't mean that we have the right to give up. The Afghans deserve a better future, just like so many others. All the shortcomings of politics, and our inability to help them, can't be seen as proof that they don't need our assistance. It doesn't give us the moral right to once again leave them in the lurch. Just because it isn't easy doesn't mean that we can just feel free to go home. Their problems and challenges are also ours. We must put greater demands on the Afghan leadership, but also on ourselves.

After dinner, Sam sits down at his post in the middle of the living room, with the curtains pulled aside so that he has a view of the garden and my only entrance. He rocks in Ikea's Poäng chair, with the arsenal of weapons laid out in a half-circle on the floor at his feet. The image could be taken straight out of some article in a tabloid about an especially successful weapons raid.

"You two go up and sleep," he says.

And I'm so deeply thankful to have friends. People to hold on to in a storm.

The next day. Kabul seems to me quieter than ever. The Ministry of Interior Affairs has set a curfew from 7 pm to 5 am, and

Nick and I confer by phone. We're wondering what to do about our party. We had planned a combined goodbye and birthday party at Jaisalmer, an Indian restaurant in Qal-e Fatullah. We had rented the whole place and ordered food for half a regiment.

"I drove by the restaurant. No party there! They've closed it and sent the staff back to India to recover."

"No one can be there anyway. The ruins of the house next door are still smoldering. Smells like crap," he continues with a dry laugh.

All this destruction. To what end? Will they never grow tired of it? Everything is so worn out here, so broken, so poor, and yet the first reaction to a problem is to destroy some more, tear down whatever has managed to rise from the ashes.

"So now what do we do? I want to have a goodbye party."

"With a curfew after seven o'clock?"

"I want a party," I insist.

Can he hear how I'm pouting? But I want to have a party.

"Of course we'll have a party."

Of course we'll arrange the deck chairs on the Titanic.

It ends up being an afternoon party in a nearby house that we borrow. Friends, acquaintances, strangers – people stream in. A party is what everyone seems to need after the past week. The feeling is wonderfully upbeat as we stand there drinking out of our beer bottles and gnawing on chicken kebab and laughing a little too loudly. We drink, make noise, and dance as if it were our last day of life. This is how I want to remember Kabul: the smell of grass and roses that tickles your nose, the hum of voices and the music that escapes through the open veranda door. I want to remember it as a long, merry, warm afternoon, evening, and night in the company of fantastic and fascinating people.

When the curfew is lifted in the early morning hours, I totter the few blocks home on heels that are too high, placing my pink stilettos carefully on the gravel road to avoid the holes. It's summer again, and the air is warm in spite of the early morning hour. The guards outside my house sit half asleep on their chairs in their dusty uniforms, with their Kalashnikovs resting on their laps.

They look just the same as they did during my first week in the country, though maybe there are a few more of them.

A few days later, a Hungarian moving company packs up my things in the biggest cartons I've ever seen. They can barely get them out when it's time to lift them; it takes several men to do it. The boxes are to be flown out by cargo plane. I wonder if I'll ever see any of it again. Does it matter? What would I miss? Of everything I drag around with me, is there anything that's truly important? Probably not.

Everything I don't want I carry out to the trash, where Najib takes care of it.

"Can I take this, Miss Diana?" he asks, holding up a rejected saucepan, or a few magazines, or a half-used notebook, or a sweater that I'm tired of.

"Yes, of course, Najib. Take what you want, please do."

On the one hand I'm happy it's being used, on the other I'm ashamed of my excess.

When the boxes have been carried out and the house is empty, I spend my last nights at Serena. Serena is a little zone of something else that's not Kabul, although it does have elegant Afghan decor. A real five-star hotel right in the heart of Kabul. It's situated near the same park as the unfinished monumental Haji Abdul Rahman mosque, which the Taliban began building with Saudi money. For years now, the abandoned building site has been sitting there like a concrete skeleton surrounded by rickety scaffolding. I like the way the two are crowded together there, a symbol of all the compromises that line the country's history. A reminder that history turns a page from time to time.

I love Serena. At Serena there's an espresso machine in the teahouse, even if no one seems able to work it and there's no fresh milk. There are clean, pressed sheets on the soft beds, and a buffet of pastries in the breakfast restaurant. Staying at Serena is perfect as a gradual phaseout, a little training for my upcoming life in Europe. Sort of like the socialization in preschool, a few hours at a time.

On my last evening in the country I have dinner with my Pakistani friend Mostafa at L'atmosphere. The food is as ghastly as always – I have a dry quiche with a few tired lettuce leaves – but the gorgeous garden makes up for everything. We drink wine, we talk about how he's going to come and visit me sometime when I'm in Stockholm, how I want to show him my hometown like he has shown me his, during a few colorful days in Lahore. I'd like to show him my city from a hot air balloon on a beautiful summer day. Aymeric, a blond, handsome Frenchman I met at a party a few months earlier, joins us, and we drink even more wine. The evening is warm, and the noise from the other tables drifts past the flower bushes to the couch where we are sitting, uncorking a third bottle, talking about Afghanistan – about what has not worked in politics and what might still be saved, about our frustration and powerlessness, about the future.

I feel melancholy and happy at the same time – melancholy about everyone I'm leaving behind, yet happy and relieved that I'm leaving. When will I see them again, all these people who are my new friends? The people that I know here know me as a different Diana from the one who walks around the streets of Stockholm. They might even know me better than the people back home, even though I know so little about them, or about who they were before they came here.

Constant meetings, constant departures. Certainly I'm going to miss them, but staying is no longer an option. I'm tired, worn out; when I look at myself in the mirror it feels like I've been here for five years, instead of barely two. I couldn't stand another winter gnawed by cold – not now, maybe sometime later, another year. Right now I need a country with central heating. *Dear God, please let Belgium have central heating!* One small consolation is that in a few more months, nothing here will be like it was anyway. Many of my close friends will have left, replaced by newly arrived diplomats and aid workers, filled with energy and conviction, advice, warnings, and confident assertions about how Afghanistan's problems should be solved. The security situation will be even worse – you don't need a crystal ball to see that – and more places will be off limits, more provinces even harder, if not life-threatening, to visit.

My own settling of accounts is simultaneously a new chapter. Leave-takings and goodbyes are part of the price that I pay for this job. They are a part of the equation, the part of the equation that I never solve, and never complete. One side of me rarely finds peace in the present; it's always on the road. But I leave a piece of my heart behind, buried in the Afghan sand. Few places, and few other people, have touched me as deeply.

The next morning, I get up early, take a hot shower, take an aspirin for my headache, and pack up the last of my things. I call the porter, who helps me drag my luggage outside: three bags with everything I need for the next three months, until my moving boxes arrive. Everything that I need to start over, again, somewhere else.

Afterword

Ever since I first arrived in Afghanistan in 2004, I've heard that Afghanistan "is at a decisive crossroads". I've read a long line of articles and reports about this crossroads, this point in time that's been reached, but never has this worn-out cliché seemed more apt than now.

As I write this, a weakened president Karzai has just emerged as the winner after a messy presidential election in Afghanistan, more than two months after the elections took place in August 2009.

The election exposed the gaps in the rickety construction of the Afghan state. The final spurt did have its bright moments, although few people will remember them: The election was preceded by an actual political debate, the many candidates campaigned across the country, there were few inter-ethnic clashes, and the complicated logistics before the election worked better than expected.

Instead, it's the bitter aftertaste that lingers, an epilogue that amused only the Taliban. The election was accompanied by massive fraud. Hundreds of polling places that only existed on paper delivered thousands of votes that were never cast, while elsewhere, nearly empty ballot boxes – participation was very low in some places – were filled with ballots. The incumbent president was quick to declare himself the winner, but was pressured to accept the fact that the Electoral Complaints Commission finally disqualified nearly one-third of his votes after two months, and took away his victory. With less than fifty percent of the votes in the first election round, another, final round was ordered between Karzai and his main opponent Abdullah Abdullah – an ophthalmologist, Tajik representative, and former foreign minister in Karzai's regime – the candidate who had achieved the second highest number of votes.

Dr. Abdullah made several demands before the second, decisive election round. Stating that he didn't want to run in an election that was as fraudulent as the first one had been, he demanded that some key ministers be replaced, a number of people suspected of orchestrating the fraud fired, ghost polling places eliminated, and the head of the not-so-independent election commission replaced. Karzai refused, and Abdullah pulled out. The election commission, which had been led by a hardcore Karzai supporter and was only nominally independent, declared the second round of voting cancelled and Karzai the winner. And thus, like a phoenix, Karzai emerged as president for yet another five years. Only the future will tell if his presidential terms will even end here. *Expect the unexpected.*

Where do we go from here? How do we work with such a scarred president? And how much influence will be wielded by the many warlords on whom Karzai depended in order to scrape together his votes?

As a colleague of Foreign Minister Carl Bildt for the past three years, I've gained new insight into the complex project of getting a war-torn country on its feet. From my new vantage point, I've seen all the efforts that are made on another level, in capitals around the world. Carl, practiced like few others, has the perspective and experience of a peace broker, and is able to see a way forward even when most things are moving backward. But it isn't easy, and there aren't any instant recipes for success, neither here nor anywhere else. And it all takes time.

So even if the challenges in Afghanistan seem bigger to me now than in 2004, I still want to believe that there's hope. The United States, which has by far the most influence, has placed Afghanistan at the top of its foreign policy agenda. The international community, which is paying for essentially the entire Afghan bill, is trying to correct the course. After eight years of dearly purchased experiences, we should be better equipped to map out the course. The tendency to shut our eyes to the many structural problems – impunity, corruption, drugs, nepotism, the influence of the warlords – has lessened. And during the years that have passed, some of the challenges that we face in Afghanistan have moved closer to home. There is a growing realization that our own democratic values are threatened, in the aftermath of terror attacks and violent controversies over freedom of expression, including the right to criticize Islam. What's happening in Afghanistan – or in Pakistan, Somalia, or Gaza – concerns us, whether we like it or not.

But the greatest responsibility lies with the Afghan leadership. The Afghan government that eventually emerges from the chaos of the elections must choose correctly at this fork in the road. In the end, it is the Afghans themselves who must build up their country. It remains to be seen if a weakened Karzai will be able to deliver what he barely managed to do earlier, under more favorable conditions: officials who serve the citizens instead of lining their own pockets; security, development, and education; strong tactics against drugs and impunity. But even with the best policies and intentions, it will take time before the results become apparent.

In any case, the pressure on Karzai and his appointed government to deliver results and change has already increased – especially the pressure from outside. Blank checks are no longer to be expected during this second mandate period.

Stockholm and Delhi, November 2009

*Thank you to Irena Busic,
Olof Ehrenkrona, Elisabet Larsdotter, Spasa Ratkovic,
Torbjörn Sohlström, Nina Wadensjö, and Ann Wilkens.
A special thank you to Professor Ulf Olsson
for years of steady encouragement.*